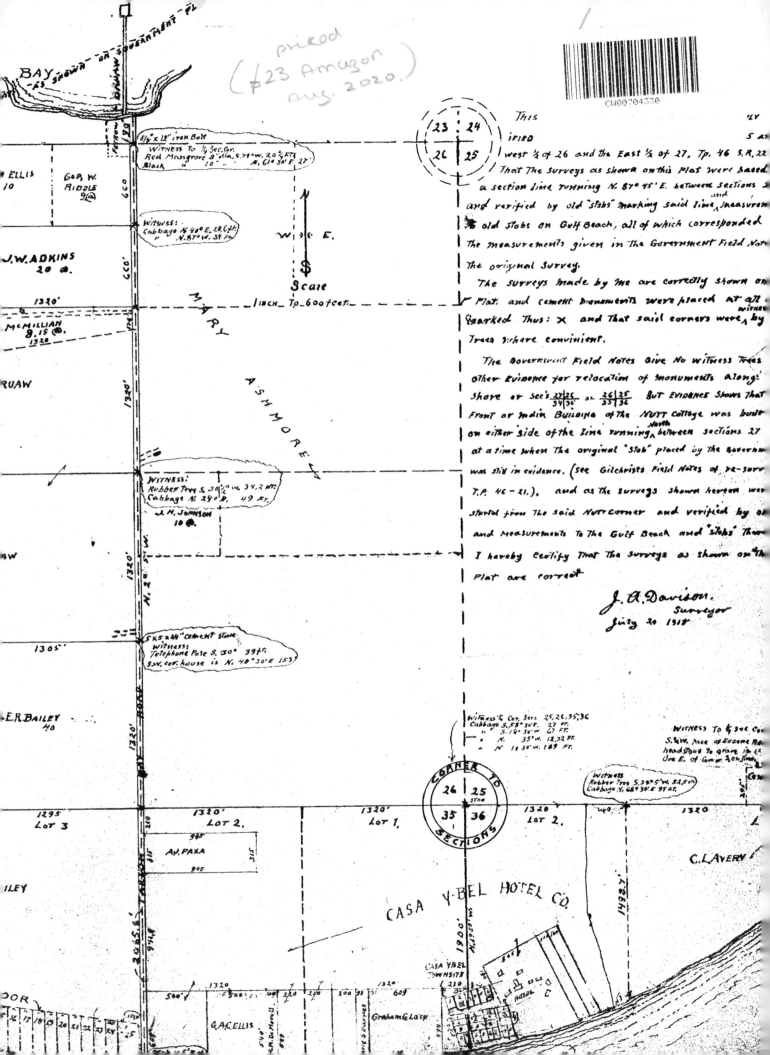

The Sanibel Historical Preservation Committee
and the
City of Sanibel
are proud to sponsor this book
on behalf of the
Sanibel Historical Village and Museum
in honor of the
City of Sanibel's 25th Anniversary

Sanibel's Story

VOICES AND IMAGES

from Calusa to Incorporation

by

Betty Anholt

Best wishes,
Betty Anholt
1-12-02

THE
DONNING COMPANY
PUBLISHERS

Copyright © 1998 by the City of Sanibel

Second printing, 2000.

All rights reserved, including the right to reproduce this work in any form whatsoever without permission in writing from the publisher, except for brief passages in connection with a review.

For information, write:

The Donning Company/Publishers
184 Business Park Drive, Suite 106
Virginia Beach, VA 23462

Steve Mull, General Manager
B. L. Walton, Jr., Project Director
Dawn V. Kofroth, Assistant General Manager
Sally C. Davis, Associate Editor
Percival Tesoro, Graphic Designer
Teri S. Arnold, Senior Marketing Coordinator
Julia Kilmer-Buitrago, Reprint Editor

Library of Congress Cataloging-in-Publication Data:

Anholt, Betty, 1943—
            Sanibel's story: voices and images from Calusa to incorporation/
      by Betty Anholt.
                        p. cm.
            Includes bibliographical references (p.) and index.
            ISBN 1-57864-046-6 (Hardcover : alk. paper)
            1. Sanibel Island (Fla.)—History. 2. Sanibel Island (Fla.)—
      History—Pictorial works. I. Title
      F317.S37A53 1998
      975.9'48—dc21
                                                      98—37822
                        CIP

Printed in the United States of America

Contents

Foreword

If a picture is worth a thousand words, then this pictorial presentation of Sanibel's history speaks volumes. Readers are able to see the rich array of Sanibel's uniqueness stretching from long-ago beginnings to events of recent vintage.

The many faces of this special barrier Island and its people brought forth in this book give testimony to the serene beauty and spectacular quality of life that are the essence of Sanibel. From nearby early Native Americans to modern-day tourists from afar, the combination of climate and coastline has captivated so many for so long. Fishing, farming, vacationing, residing, working, and playing all made the mosaic, with Mother Nature as the constant. Her beauty and her power have always dominated.

Hurricanes and mosquitoes have been awesome—and changed life. The Great Storm of 1926 effectively ended the agriculture and packing house entrepreneurs of the time. Hurricanes are still "out there" to be reckoned with, but spraying, air conditioning, and water management have reduced mosquitoes to a relatively minor irritant.

Probably the two most significant events of the past fifty years were manmade—the construction of the Causeway (1963) and the advent of Home Rule (1974). The first opened the way for a trickle of development that soon threatened to be a flood; the second involved a remarkably successful display of grassroots democracy and debate in a spirited community determined to preserve its unique identity.

As the twentieth century winds down, the allure of Sanibel continues as strong and unabated as a full jasmine bloom on a still warm night. More and more have discovered Sanibel and more and more are discovering it every day through the wonder of modern technology and travel—and of course, the Causeway. Equally, every day the machinery of Home Rule—the City of Sanibel—gears up to handle the challenges of all the growth. As long as the City succeeds in its Charter Mandate to preserve forever the beautiful natural resources and unique quality of life, pressure to grow will intensify. Success is seldom easy and often short-lived.

So the New Millennium begins for Sanibel with the knowledge that there will continue to be a tension between our preservation and pressure for new growth. The people of Sanibel who have collectively helped evolve Sanibel into the spectacular place it is today were well guided by looking back to yesterday. Some wonderful glimpses of that yesterday are provided here—so you can better understand why Sanibel is so special and should remain so.

Porter Goss

Porter Goss served on Sanibel's Council from its 1974 inception until 1982. He was Sanibel's first Mayor, and served four separate one-year terms in that position. He is currently representing southwest Florida's Fourteenth District as its U.S. Congressman. (Courtesy *Islander*)

Acknowledgments

Every generation should tell the next one about its ancestors.
Mario Sanchez
Key West primitive painter

Generations of islanders have seen themselves as an extended family. Not always related by blood, we have been related by our reliance on each other and our isolation from the rest of the world. Although that isolation has weakened in recent times, it shaped Sanibel's cultural past as surely as the sea shaped our shores. This collective family album gives a glimpse of the people and times that have evolved into today's Sanibel.

An extraordinary number of people have held memories of Sanibel dear and shared them with the Sanibel Historical Museum. Residents, descendants of island pioneers, and visitors have kept stories and letters, photos and memorabilia safe. By protecting their thread of Sanibel's history they allow us to know islanders who are now gone. All history is a kind of story-telling, whether formal or word-of-mouth, and to hear the voices from the past is to open a door to their time. Those who gathered and safeguarded this treasure, and then shared it, give us a precious understanding of our place and ourselves.

The Sanibel Historical Preservation Committee first discussed this book in 1995. Jody Brown had the inspiration to tie it to the 25th Anniversary of the City of Sanibel. Committee members in 1995 were Sam Bailey—Chairman, Boyd Anderson, Harry Bertossa, Jody Brown, Jean Downes, Warren Deuber, Sarah Fallert, Milbrey Rushworth and John Veenschoten.

The Sanibel Public Library began taking oral histories of long-term residents in the late 1960s on audiotape. Today the program continues as a joint library-museum project, with transcriptions and videotape added. Thirty years of unsung "middlemen" have recorded, transcribed, and protected documents, photos and memories. Sanibel's reference librarian, Cheryl Morales, has been exceptionally interested and helpful at many stages of the book. Reference librarians throughout the state, and as far away as New York and Indiana, have unfailingly provided information and clues to the story.

Thank you everyone, anonymous and named, including Pat Allen (*Sanibel Public Library*), Hazel Amon, Kristie Anders (*Sanibel-Captiva Conservation Foundation*), Cameron Anholt, Jim Anholt, Francis Bailey, Mary Bell, Anne Bellew, Gertrude Bergin, Barbara Billheimer, Roger Blind and Lori Thompson (*Island Water Association*), Carol Branyon (*J. N. "Ding" Darling National Wildlife Refuge*), Carlene Brennen, Jean Brock, Eleanor and Don Brown, Gil Bursley, Paul Camp (*University of South Florida Special Collections*), Clement Concordora (*Priscilla Murphy Realty*), Jean Culpepper, Anne Daves, Elinore Dormer, Bob and Mae England, Carol Ehrlich, Bruce and Barbara Frazier, Debbie Frederick (*Bailey-Matthews Shell Museum*), Porter Goss, Sara Nell Gran (*Southwest Florida Historical Society*), Tom Hambright (*Monroe County Library—Florida Reference*), Marjorie Harris, Bill Hicks (*Sanibel Community Association*), Historical Association of South Florida, Marty and Mary Holtz, Dick Jacker, Carl and Mozella Jordan, Robin Hunter Karr, Polly King Kimball, Charles and Jean LeBuff, Ethel Longmire, Christy Loucks, Scott Martell (*Islander*), Ron McCoy, Charles and Ann McCullough, Jeannine Mendolusky, Michelle Moran and Gwenda Hiett-Clements (*Island Reporter*), Allen and Goldie Nave, Carol Nix, Dick Noon, Bill Opp and Mary Sullivan (*Lee County Mosquito Control*), Evelyn Pearson, Jim and Jo Pickens, Jim and Suzanne Pickens, Elaine Pike (*Vassar College Library*), Vivian Pyke, Sallie Rich, Julia Dickey Scott, Jeany Smusz, Linda Uhler, John and Muriel Veenschoten, Jo Ann Wagner, Charlotte Kinzie White, Betty Williamson, Frances Willis, Ann Wollschlager, Ralph Woodring, Nick Wynne (*Florida Historical Society Library*), and Florence Young.

A meld of perception and fact, no history can be entirely complete or accurate, although that goal is what one endeavors to reach. Any errors are wholly my responsibility. Photographs not credited within the captions have been donated to the Sanibel Historical Village and Museum in the years previous to creating this book.

Fashionable beach attire for bathing or shelling in 1912.

Vaughnie Rhodes and Fritz, the lighthouse cat, at the Sanibel Light in the late 1920s. Vaughnie's sister Lula was married to Roscoe (Mac) McClane, who was Assistant Keeper and Lighthouse Keeper until 1938.

This 1957 aerial illustrates Sanibel's geology. The numerous parallel ridges and swales formed as the island built to the south and east. Sabal palmetto grows on ridges, the spartina and saw grasses in swales, and deeper swales hold water. Casa Ybel is at the lower left, Tarpon Bay top left, and the pathway to Reed's Landing is distinct at the top through what is today the Dunes subdivision. Dixie Beach Boulevard doesn't yet exist. The central line of Australian pines marks the main road, later named Periwinkle Way. (Courtesy Priscilla Murphy Realty)

Chapter One

Ten thousand years ago the place we have named Sanibel was part of a much wider Florida. From the intersection of Periwinkle and Causeway Roads it might have been as much as one hundred miles to the beach. A few thousand years later, that same intersection would be covered by the Gulf of Mexico.

About five thousand years ago, when the environment stabilized to the conditions we recognize today, a small sea-washed islet remained above water, and

Before the Lighthouse

(pre-1884)

long-shore currents deposited sand grains year after year. The islet grew toward the south and east as sea levels and storms willed.

Sanibel's emergence from the sea corresponds to that of many barrier islands, but even in its geology Sanibel is unusual. Where most barrier islands are narrow and parallel to the coast, Sanibel curves voluptuously out to sea, a characteristic noted by mariners from the earliest times. Long before the Sanibel Light beckoned, the island itself was a marker for the sailor.

The reason for Sanibel's curving shape may relate to bedrock formed a million or more years ago. Geologists have traced a faultline across the lower end of the island, up the Caloosahatchee, the northwestern side of Lake Okeechobee, and out into the Atlantic. This fault, no longer active, helped shape south Florida's geology.

As Sanibel developed, a series of dune ridges and overwash swales formed. From the air, these delineate the island's growth in clear lap marks akin to the lines left by retreating waves on today's beach. Vegetation started to colonize bare sand, rain puddled between dune ridges, insects and birds foraged, and eventually loggerheads, crabs, and wandering mammals came.

Native Americans were early visitors, no doubt attracted by oyster bars, fish, turtle, and other food resources. Visits led to settlements, and in the oldest part of the island, near the exit from J. N. "Ding" Darling National Wildlife Refuge, archaeologists have documented Indian habitation as much as 2300 years ago. It is likely that offshore many underwater sites, drowned by rising sea levels, hold clues to Sanibel's human population millennia past.

When the Spanish first came to the New World at the close of the fifteenth century, the Indians on Sanibel were Calusa. The waterways of Pine Island Sound, Charlotte Harbor, and Estero Bay behind Fort Myers Beach were central

Archaeology volunteers at the Wightman site, near Wulfert, 1974. Although Sanibel was rich in Indian remains, many have eroded or been hauled away for roadfill. The Wightman dig examined environmental characteristics as well as artifacts, and is often cited as an archaeological model in Florida. Wightman's first confirmed occupation dates to 300 B.C.

Juan Ponce de Leon, from a drawing in Herrera.

for the tribe, the most powerful Florida Indians of the time. Indian towns on both coasts from Sarasota and Cape Canaveral to the Keys and throughout the interior paid tribute to the Calusa.

Politically savvy, the chief or head cacique of the Calusa manipulated the Spanish to obtain not only goods but backing in their disputes with distant tribes. When pressed to convert to Catholicism, the Calusa did so freely, as long as gifts of corn and cloth continued. They were happy to add another God to their pantheon, although they refused to renounce their own. If the gifts stopped, the Spanish clerics found themselves ignored or humiliated. In 1697 several priests summoned by the Calusa who had failed to bring gifts were not only mocked and run out of town, but stripped of all their clothing.

The Calusa society was a ranked one. The head cacique was called king by the Spanish. In addition to the royals, whose position was hereditary, and their advisors, Calusa society was divided into several ranks of artisans, general populace, and slaves. Some physical remains of their mound and canal-building society can still be seen on Sanibel and Captiva, but their major towns were on Pine Island, Mound Key, and other nearby islands.

The Calusa had become a powerful group because of the abundance of resources in southwest Florida. Living was indeed easy, as food was plentiful. Trade with other tribes produced wealth, and free time to specialize. The Calusa were water people, great divers, canal builders, and fishermen. They stored fish and turtle in pens and weirs, and allowed the tides to work for them. Their engineering and artistic skills are only beginning to be discerned and appreciated.

As politicians they were unexcelled—subtle and devious, they outwitted the Spanish time after time. The Calusa leader held the secrets which "caused the fish to swim," so if the plenitude diminished he was held accountable by his subjects. He and his advisors, religious and civil, had much responsibility along with their power, and held daily councils to ensure the tribe's livelihood remained in balance.

The first meeting of Spaniard and Calusan of which we have written confirmation occurred in 1513, the Florida discovery voyage of Juan Ponce de Leon. Somewhere in the vicinity of San Carlos Bay, perhaps on the beach of Sanibel, that expedition met a Spanish-speaking Indian. The Indian's knowledge of Spanish meant some earlier contact, probably illegal slaving raids, had occurred.

The 1513 expedition lingered at Sanibel about three weeks. It was May, and Ponce's ships had been sailing in tropical waters for nearly three months. Never agile, the ships had accumulated so much marine growth on their wooden hulls that they barely made headway. Sanibel's shallow waters and gentle shoreline slope allowed Ponce's vessels to be careened—tipped onto their sides and cleaned of the barnacles, algae, and encrusting material that slowed the ships so dramatically. While this went on, the Spanish and Calusa made contact before the vessels sailed away.

Juan Ponce de Leon kept Sanibel in mind. Eight years later he attempted to establish a colony on Florida's west coast, and the spot he chose was San Carlos Bay. If it had succeeded this would have been the first European settlement in the present limits of the United States. In 1521 he arrived here with two hundred colonists—farmers and clerics—and many horses, cattle, pigs, sheep, farming implements and seeds. As the group began the process of building their settlement, probably at Punta Rassa across from Sanibel, the Calusa became aware of the activity. To them, the settlement was a direct threat, and they attacked, routing the Spanish in a battle which killed about eighty-five. Ponce de Leon was wounded in the thigh. The arrow point evidently lodged in the bone and couldn't be removed. Ten days after the battle he died in Havana, where the group had precipitously retreated. It seems likely he died of infection from the wound. The Calusa reputation for fierceness was underlined. Later explorers like Narvaez and de Soto prudently traveled farther up the peninsula before coming ashore.

Although the name Sanibel is probably corrupted from the Spanish, it first appeared on a map dated 1765, during the English control of Florida. Exploring and naming bodies of water and passes tended to be more important to sailors than land masses. Cautivo Pass, now Captiva Pass, and Ponce Bay, now San Carlos Bay, are early examples on charts. Indeed, the Sanibel name relates to piloting—Sanibel historian Elinore Dormer points out that S. Nivel means south level, and allows the sailor to pinpoint the deep water behind the island's eastern point.

The English acquired Florida in 1763 through the Treaty of Paris. They had captured Havana the year before, and the Spanish traded Florida to regain possession of that city. Few Indians were left in Florida. Old World disease such as smallpox or measles had destroyed more Indians than European swords. Florida Indians had developed relationships with the Spanish over time and did not trust the English. They, many Calusa among them, retreated to the Keys and left for Havana during the English period. Cuba was a familiar place to the Calusa as travel and trade via dugout canoe to Cuba had been ongoing for centuries.

Cuban fishermen had been coming north to fish, and often employed Indians at their fishing ranchos. The Cubans dried and salted mullet during the winter season, living in palmetto houses at their processing stations. These fishing ranchos existed from the late 1600s to about 1900 throughout Charlotte Harbor, notably on Cayo Costa, Useppa, Captiva, Punta Rassa, and Sanibel.

England returned Florida to the Spanish in 1783 following the American Revolution. Fishing continued, probably the longest consistent human tradition in southwest Florida. The Calusa were gone, except possibly the occasional "Spanish Indian" at a fishing rancho. Florida was empty of its native population.

The quiet of Sanibel's estuary waters would be influenced by distant events. A new foreign country, the United States of America, had emerged to the north. As it grew and flexed its muscles, it pushed Indian tribes west and south. Where the Spanish lived and worked with the Indians, the English and Americans only wanted them gone. Their focus was the land, not human souls. Disorganized remnants of southeast Indian tribes regrouped in Spanish Florida. These wanderers or runaways from their homelands became known as Seminoles. First establishing themselves in Spanish north Florida, they continued streaming south as Americans spilled into Florida, once more forcing them off their lands.

After raids by Andrew Jackson and others, Spain realized they could never maintain Florida as a Spanish possession. In 1821 Florida became a territory of the United States. Previous to the turnover, numerous land grants within Florida had been given by the Spanish king. These and other privately owned lands were to remain with their owners, but apart from those the United States acquired vast lands.

Suddenly Cuban fishing ranchos were working in a foreign land. Worse still, Americans saw that the "foreign" fishermen, who had been established in Charlotte Harbor for hundreds if not thousands of years, were making money that Americans could be making. The land their ranchos were on was American. They were squatters without proof of residency or ownership rights. The process of opening the area to American commerce had begun.

Key West was established in 1822. It became a base and major jumping-off point for Florida exploration. One Spanish land grant, the Alagon Grant, had been subdivided by the Grantee, the Duke of Alagon, in 1819. A portion was given to Richard S. Hackley, earlier the United States Consul in Spain. The lands Hackley claimed included one-half of a huge swath from the mouth of the St. Johns River (north of present Jacksonville) to the St. Lucia River (near the present town of Stuart), and to the Gulf of Mexico and its islands. This included Charlotte Harbor and Sanibel. Less than a dozen years after Florida had become an American possession, Hackley sold an interest to the Florida Land Company, a New York development company, and began surveying and subdividing Sanibel. Hackley's land claims were disputed by the United States from the start, but he didn't wait for the court to rule in his favor. Indeed the issue was not finally resolved until 1905, when the Hackley claim was denied.

In the meantime, Sanibel's first European settlers came north from Key West. In January of 1833 about forty people came to the island, where five large palmetto houses had been constructed by Cubans for them near the eastern point. Over the next several months they built several wooden houses, at least one which was of two stories. Author John Lee Williams reported that by 1837 the settlement had been destroyed. Uncertainty about the validity of the land ownership or simple isolation and mosquitoes could have been factors, but the beginning of the bloody Second Seminole Indian War in late 1835 sealed the settlement's fate. In 1836 not a single person resided anywhere in all of Charlotte Harbor. Even the Cubans on the fishing ranchos deserted when the resident U.S. Customs Inspector Henry Crews was murdered on Useppa Island, although his death may have been more related to his autocratic attitude than the Indian uprisings.

The 1833 settlers were the first to request a lighthouse for Sanibel, addressing a "Petition to the Secretary of the Treasury by Residents of the Island of Sanybel" in December 1833.

Dr. Benjamin B. Strobel, who had gone to Key West from his native Charleston, was an army post surgeon and published the Key West newspaper. He was fascinated by Florida and wrote a series of articles on his explorations. When Audubon visited the Florida Keys in 1832 he frequently consulted with Strobel. The doctor, who came to the island with the others in January 1833, described their adventures reaching the island and running aground on a sand bank in sight of Sanibel, where they "lay thumping for several hours the sea occasionally sweeping our decks."

When they landed in the morning they were "assailed by immense swarms of flees [sic], whose company we could well have dispensed with." The "flees" were blamed on the Cuban fishermen. That night a storm produced "thirty or forty beautiful little streams of water . . . rushing through our lodging, with a delightful murmurring [sic] noise. In a few minutes we were all afloat, our bed room being converted into a complete lake."

The next morning while wading up the fresh water branch we know as the Sanibel River, he "happened to get on top of an old Alligator which was lying on the bottom, he flirted, floundered, and cleared himself." As did Strobel, who decided not to wade the stream any more.

He shot blue-wing teal, saw wild pigs on Captiva, and visited the Punta Rassa fishing rancho where he had an "excellent supper." Later in the evening the rancho put on a Ball, dancing the Spanish fandango and another dance performed by the Indian women alone. He was presented with a handful of "splendid Spanish seegars" and spent the night.

Benjamin B. Strobel described 1833 Sanibel.
(Courtesy Florida Historical Society)

In 1838 Fort Dulaney was established at Punta Rassa, probably on the site of the rancho Strobel visited. From it soldiers explored Sanibel and other islands, but the fort was destroyed by a tremendous hurricane in October 1841, killing two soldiers and forcing everyone into the trees to save themselves. The steamer *Isis* was "high and dry in the middle of the camp," some twelve to fifteen feet above sea level. Sanibel must have been totally underwater. The fort was moved upriver, and Sanibel continued to be left deserted. The Third Indian War and the Civil War passed, and Confederate cattle were smuggled by Sanibel's shores but not until after the War Between the States was over did the island again see any attempt to settle.

In 1867 the underwater telegraph cable line to Key West and Havana was laid from Punta Rassa to Havana. The cable crossed the eastern tip of Sanibel before it reached Punta Rassa, and an 1888 map indicates two telegraph cable huts, one bayside and one on the Gulf side of the island.

Probably about the time these buildings were erected, William S. Allen and his son George arrived to farm. William was a Connecticut Yankee, first coming to Florida in 1852. He and his family moved to Key West ten years later, where his brother was a wholesale merchant. They became partners. He and his son probably came from there to farm on Sanibel. Key West was the county seat of Monroe County, and Sanibel was still a part of that county. The Allens farmed castor beans, and many grow on the island today. The oil was used in machinery and medicine. In 1870 William Allen served as census-taker and Assistant Marshall, and listed only his sixteen-year-old son and himself as residing on "Sinnabel Island." A major hurricane in 1873 probably discouraged their efforts, and William Allen later bought up and developed what is now Everglades City. The Barron River was first named Allen River for him. William became mayor of Key West, and died there in 1891, a prominent citizen of the town.

The "Barracks" was built during the Third Seminole War on the Punta Rassa site of Fort Dulaney. It became a hotel operated by George Schultz when the International Ocean Telegraph Company took it over in 1867. (Courtesy Historical Museum of Southern Florida)

Probably Sanibel's oldest building before its destruction during a controlled burn on refuge land in 1992, the cable hut acted as a junction box for the underwater cable laid in 1867 from Havana to Punta Rassa. The cable ran across Sanibel's eastern tip on the lighthouse reservation en route to the mainland.

Sanibel historian Elinore Dormer points out remnants of the telegraph cable which ran from Havana to Punta Rassa, where it crossed Sanibel, then San Carlos Bay. The cable, laid in 1867, ran 133 miles underwater from Key West to Punta Rassa, and weighed one and a quarter tons per mile. Its core of seven strands of fine copper wire was surrounded by three layers of gutta percha (a rubbery, tropical tree latex), a covering of hemp, and lead armor. The shore ends were even heavier at two tons per mile. The run from Key West to Cuba was 102 miles. Although plagued by frequent breaks, it was a technological achievement and operated until 1942.

"On shore there was a bedlam of sounds, the bellowing of penned cattle, the cries of drovers, the barking of dogs, the cracking of drags. The drag is a very heavy and long whip, sometimes eighteen feet in length and with a very short handle. . . . As night drew on the noise increased. Bonfires and torches flared in the darkness. Bellowing herds came pouring in from the backwoods, until, at nine o'clock five hundred cattle were ready to be transferred to the steamer."

A. H. Curtis
THE BARTOW INFORMANT, November 24, 1883
[describing Summerlin's Punta Rassa cattle wharf]

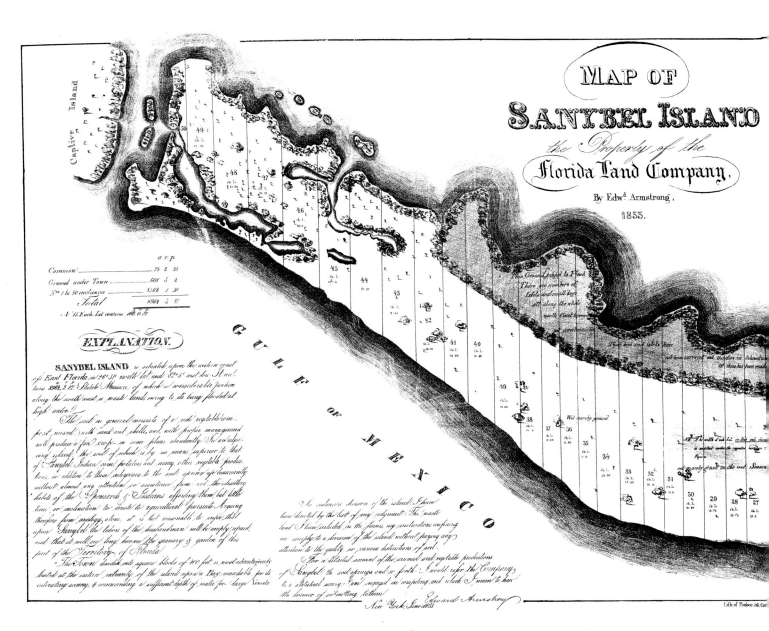

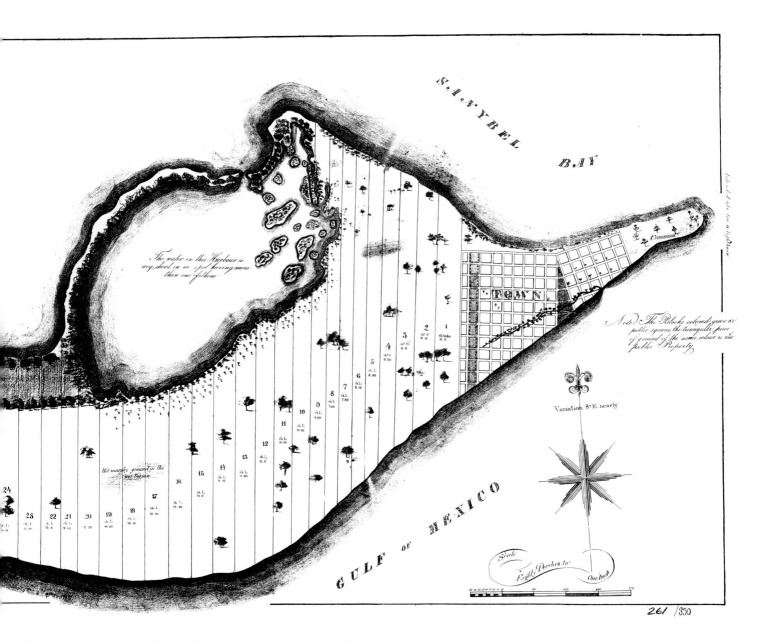

Eighteen thirty-three map of Sanybel Island, surveyed for the Florida Land Company by Edward Armstrong. Note the numerous geological features mapped, including the Sanibel River and its mouth into the Gulf of Mexico, Ladyfinger Lake in eastern Tarpon Bay, the Wulfert Keys, and Kesson (or Bowen) and Holloway Bayous to the west, as well as the configuration of the Blind Pass islands and bayous. (Courtesy Betty Williamson)

Castor beans still grow wild on Sanibel more than a century after they were first planted as a commercial crop. (Courtesy Betty Anholt)

Requests for a lighthouse on Sanibel had been ignored for various reasons—war, a restructuring of the Lighthouse Board, more war. But in 1883 plans were drawn. Cattle shipping from Punta Rassa to Havana and other ports was active, and the telegraph line linked the trickle of new residents to the world. The bay was shallow, and the light was necessary to aid navigation. War threats had diminished, and tourists were beginning to explore the watery expanses of south Florida. Excitement grew about natural resources in terms of homesteading and economics as well as sightseeing and sporting encounters with the tropical wilderness.

Penned cattle waiting to be loaded on board ship in 1912.

Jake Summerlin, the "King of the Crackers." (Courtesy Fort Myers Historical Museum)

Remains of the Summerlin House shortly before its collapse in 1982. (Courtesy Betty Anholt)

In April of 1883 Congress approved $50,000 for the Sanibel Light, and in August Florida relinquished its state claim to the island under the Swamp and Overflowed Lands Act. The construction contract was signed with the Phoenix Iron Company of Trenton, New Jersey, builder of other iron Florida Lights. Fifty years after the first request for a lighthouse on Sanibel, the tower would rise.

When the skeleton light tower and two living quarters were built in 1884, Dudley Richardson and John Johnson came from Key West to be the first Sanibel lighthouse keeper and assistant. They were alone on the island, which was wholly a government reservation. The third-order lens was first lit on August 20, 1884, a fixed white light with a white flash, standing ninety-eight feet above the ground, powered by kerosene oil. It could be seen in good visibility fifteen and three-quarter miles away.

Jacob Summerlin believed he was the first American baby born in Florida, being born in 1821 shortly after Florida became a territory of the United States. A Confederate sympathizer during the American War Between the States, he ran thousands of cattle through Union blockade lines for the South. After the Civil War, Summerlin began shipping cattle to Cuba from Punta Rassa, becoming wealthy in the process, although he never changed his rustic lifestyle. Summerlin owned a thousand acres at Punta Rassa, with cattle pens, docks, and the Summerlin House built in 1874. Although cattle shipments peaked in the 1870s, schooners and steamers loaded cattle at Punta Rassa until well into the twentieth century. In 1910 a Punta Rassa schoolteacher described the cattlemen driving their herds back into the swamps away from the water to protect them when they realized a hurricane was approaching. Shipping operations such as Summerlin's increased pressure for the lighthouse to be erected.

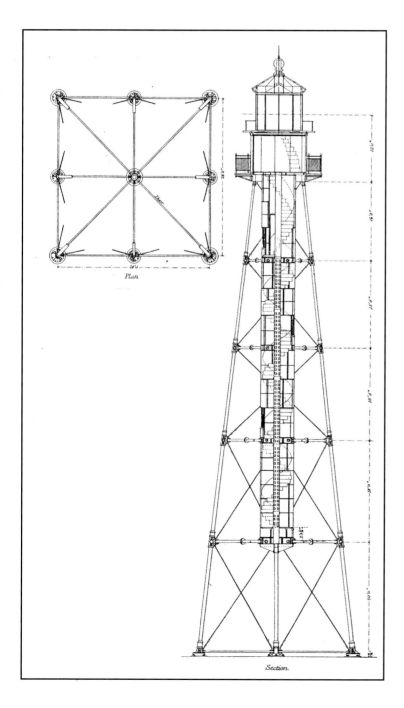

Plan.

Section.

Lighthouse section, May 1883. Cast iron disks distribute the weight of the tower columns where they meet the ground on its twenty-eight foot square base. (Courtesy National Archives)

An 1890s group fishes with handlines and a grains from the dock as their dog watches. Most of the catch is sheepshead, abundant near pilings, especially in winter. A grains is a spearlike implement with barbed forked tips, used similarly to a harpoon or gig, for impaling fish. (Courtesy Jean Brock)

Chapter Two

Wharf construction began in February 1884 on the bay side of Point Ybel to allow lighthouse construction materials to be brought ashore. The Light House Board required the iron skeleton tower to be assembled at the iron works before shipment. This made certain all the components were accurate, allowing the tower to be reassembled quickly on-site. Just two miles off Point

Early Years and Homesteading

(1884–1894)

Ybel the loaded schooner hit a sand bank and tipped, spilling the parts into the bay. All but two gallery brackets were retrieved by divers from the lighthouse tenders *Arbutus* and *Mignonette*. The brackets were easily replaced. The mishap did not delay the project and the light first guided boats into the harbor on August 20, 1884.

The following year in Tarpon Bay New Yorker W. H. Wood caught a ninety-three-pound tarpon on a rod and reel, a feat previously not thought possible. The publicity went international, attracting sports fishermen and tourists. Hotels at St. James City and Punta Rassa began to attract sportsmen and yachts began to cruise the waters in winter. Although cattle shipping and commercial fishing at the Cuban ranchos continued to be important, wealthy visitors arrived in increasing numbers to explore the subtropical wonders of the area—hunting, fishing, botanizing, and speculating on the aboriginal remains hidden in the mangroves.

The year 1888 saw a significant change on Sanibel. The federal government opened much of the island to homesteading on July 3, reserving only the east end for lighthouse purposes. The keepers of the light would become less isolated. Homesteaders could claim as much as a quarter-section, 160 acres of public land. Necessary qualifications included U.S. citizenship, being a head of household or age twenty-one, and one "who has never borne arms against the United States Government or given aid and comfort to its enemies." After registering the claim, the homesteader was required to settle and cultivate for five years without leaving more than six months. Within the following two years two credible witnesses had to prove the claim to the Land Office. Many of Sanibel's homesteaders were veterans of the Civil War. Others who came to the island in the first population wave were ship captains, preachers, retirees and sometimes refugees from troubled lives in search of a new start. Some had simply fallen in love with the island.

So Sanibel's first homesteaders became farmers. Although many crops were experiments, tomatoes and peppers soon became staple crops. Citrus groves were laid out. In the *Fort Myers Press* an 1895 visitor rhapsodized, "The prairie is beautiful, with its carpet of green, dotted here and there by stately palmettos, and covered with a profusion of beautiful wild flowers. If the famous DeLeon crossed the Sanibel prairie it must have been there that he decided upon the name of Florida (Land of Flowers)." Breaking the sod to plant was simple, even with only a mule and a few family members. Docks and bulkheads were built to accommodate freight vessels which hauled produce to the rail head at Punta Gorda or distant markets. Often the farmer doubled as a captain, like Captain George Cooper or Captain William Reed. The wondrous delicacy of Sanibel tomatoes in winter in New York City guaranteed top dollar, and the farming community prospered.

Henry Shanahan brought his wife and seven children from Key West to become Sanibel's second assistant lighthouse keeper, replacing John Johnson in 1890. When Dudley Richardson left as keeper in 1892, Shanahan was first passed over for the top job because he did not read or write. But fully-qualified keepers were not interested in the isolated post, and the job became his.

By late 1894, Sanibel was well established. Fishermen, tourists—and the "drummers"—men who brokered the sales of the farm crops—who came to the island all needed a place to stay and dinner to eat. Several farmers rented out rooms or cottages to winter visitors the way Anna Woodring did at the Woodring House.

A cold front swept over Florida as the year closed, severely damaging citrus and other crops. In Lee County, although the freeze was significant, citrus survived. Six weeks after the December freeze, a second "blue norther" killed citrus that had reestablished growth throughout Florida. Farmers from central Florida and Georgia looked south from the ruins of their fields, and many saw Sanibel.

The small steamer *Alice Howard* ran from Fort Myers to Punta Gorda from 1886 to 1900, connecting to H. B. Plant's Florida Southern Railroad to bring visitors to the islands. (Courtesy Historical Museum of Southern Florida)

"I think it would be a very pleasant trip to come down here in winter, and stay until April as the birds do. I saw some old friends here in the robins, blackbirds, sparrows, redwings, swallows and larks."

Charles A. Dean
February 2, 1888 letter (in FLORIDA'S VANISHING ERA by Eleanor H. D. Pearse, 1947)

Ironwork railings forged by Sam Woodring Sr. at the San Carlos Hotel in St. James City. This 1889 photo shows a "herdic," which transported guests from dock to hotel. A herdic is a horse-drawn cab entered from the rear, having side seats. (Courtesy Historical Museum of Southern Florida)

The original Woodring homestead was built with lumber ordered from Key West on land they had picked out even before the island was officially declared open for homesteading on July 3, 1888. The Pennsylvania family had come to St. James City on Pine Island about 1885 when the builders of the San Carlos Hotel advertised for an iron worker. Sam Woodring Sr. had become acquainted with the area while serving during the Civil War. The Woodrings were in their Sanibel home by November of 1888. When Sam Sr. died in 1899, his widow Anna operated the Woodring House, catering to Sanibel visitors. At left are a Mr. Gooddell, George Underhill, and Allie Collins. The entire Woodring homesteading family stands to the right—son Carl, daughter Flora, Mrs. Sam (Anna) Woodring, daughter Annie, Sam Jr., and Sam Sr. with Harrison, the youngest.

Flora Sanibel Woodring Morris was born in January 1889 on Middle Point—soon known as Woodring Point for her homesteading family. She was Sanibel's first-born non-Indian child, and married John E. Morris, a Sanibel farmer, in 1911. The Woodrings called the point Crescent Beach because of its lovely shape and white sand.

"I must say we didn't get over on the Gulf side very much. . . . you couldn't get there. It was too desolate, you know."

Flora Sanibel Woodring Morris
1972 Interview

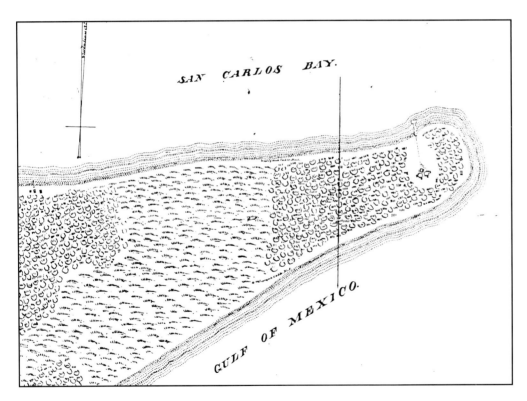

This January 1888, Light House Engineer survey of Sanibel's eastern point shows the lighthouse dock, quarters, and tower, and indicates two telegraph cable huts, one on the Gulf, one bayside. The three buildings and dock at top may be a Padillo fishing rancho as homesteading did not open on Sanibel until July 1888. (Courtesy University of South Florida, Special Collections)

The Reverend George O. Barnes and wife Jean home-steaded on the Gulf side of the island, as did their two daughters Georgia and Marie, and son William. Barnes was sailing by in 1889 when his boat grounded on a sand bar. While waiting for the tide to release him, he waded ashore, found that homesteading was available, and fell in love with the island. When he returned to Kentucky, he used his evangelistic skills to persuade a multitude of other Kentuckians to come to Sanibel. A newspaper article in 1895 reported about forty families lived on Sanibel, and listed a dozen or more who had homesteaded from the state of Kentucky. (Courtesy Jean Brock)

Palm Ranch, a stilt house, was the first home which the Barnes family erected. It was reached by two ladders visible to the rear of the building. The several ladies on the porch must have dreaded the climb in their long skirts. (Courtesy Jean Brock)

"[T]here was one dog, that I think my father had to shoot it because a rattlesnake bit it under the house."

Carrie Reed Ebsworth
1992 Interview

23

William C. Barnes holds a large yellow rat snake by a Sanibel cart path. The outer ruts are made by cartwheels, the center rut by the mule or horse. (Courtesy Jean Brock)

Marie Barnes is surrounded by family pictures, many decorated with pansies, her favorite flower. (Courtesy Jean Brock)

Bowen barn.

Oliver Bowen made his homestead at the north end of Sanibel, sailing from Trinidad where he had met and married his wife, Mary Dos Santos. Bowen was a Confederate veteran and a Mississippi riverboat pilot. In his piloting years he had been a hero to his younger cousins and their companion Samuel Clemens (Mark Twain), who later drew on the dashing Bowen's exploits in several of his books. Bowen had brought numerous agave plants from Trinidad to Sanibel, and they grow wild today on the island. He consulted with Thomas Edison, possibly about the agave's fiber. He did not profit from it however. Mary said the only time he made money on Sanibel was when he killed a rattlesnake and sold the skin. Bowen had become a bit eccentric by the time they moved to Sanibel, spending most of his time in a hammock strung between palm trees over his well. He died in 1894, leaving Mary and their three children to prove up the homestead claim. Bowen asked that he be buried in his well, so a neighbor widened it to accommodate the coffin and the request. Once Mary had secured the homestead, an older Bowen son from a previous marriage came to the island to claim his inheritance. He sent Mary and four-year-old Albert to Trinidad, Mary's daughter and other son to a northern Bowen relative for schooling, and leased the land.

Mary Dos Santos Bowen.

Pastor Andrew Wiren, an early Sanibel homesteader, was a native of Sweden. While living in Maine, he contracted tuberculosis, and could not preach or teach. Hearing that he could homestead on a healthy island, the family moved to Sanibel. One early Casa Ybel brochure claimed the name Sanibel meant "healthy and beautiful." The Wirens first lived in a thatched house on San Carlos Bay before building inland. Wiren continued to decline and died in 1890. He was buried on his property, which was later owned by the Rutlands and now is part of Periwinkle Park Campground.

Abia Wiren completed homestead requirements when her husband died, then returned to Maine with their four children.

Sam Ellis lived on Tarpon Bay's south shore. A former British Navy man, he married Safia Underhill, a tall part-Indian woman with two boys, and spent much of his time drifting on Tarpon Bay, often with a jug. The Ellises directed the archaeologist Frank Cushing to Indian sites near their home, one of which had turned up a dozen Indian skulls when they planted their garden.

Commodore Edwin Reed (left) settled on the west shore of Tarpon Bay about the same time as his neighbors, the Woodrings, homesteaded the eastern mouth of the bay. He built his house with palmetto leaves in the manner of the fishing ranchos and tended fruit trees and bananas, living on a Navy pension. Commodore Creek leading into Tarpon Bay commemorates his homesite. His neighbor Sam Ellis visits with him.

Captain George Madison Cooper claimed his home was the island's first post office since he would pick up Sanibel's mail at St. James City and deposit it on his wife's sewing machine for other islanders to pick up. The *Fort Myers Press* reported that Cooper, who homesteaded on Tarpon Bay Road, shipped one-third of the thousand crates of tomatoes leaving Sanibel one week in 1894.

"Mr. G. M. Cooper of Sanibel will begin shipping tomatoes this week. The deer have been eating up a large quantity of tomatoes for Messrs. Cooper, Collins, & Bailey and they are afraid they will have hard work to put a stop to it. They have only succeeded killing one of the 'varmints' so far, though they have used every endeavor."

Fort Myers Press
April 25, 1895

Laetitia Lafon Ashmore Nutt, wife of Confederate Captain LeRoy Moncure Nutt, circa 1860.

Laetitia Nutt arrived here from her adopted state of Louisiana in 1889 with three daughters, Cordie, Lettie, and Nannie; a brother, James Ashmore; and her mother-in-law, Ann Moncure Taliaferrow Nutt; after hearing from fellow Kentuckian Reverend Barnes that homesteading opportunities existed on a beautiful island. She built the still-existing farm house which would later be called Gray Gables. A widow with a strong backbone and opinions who had suffered several reverses, Mrs. Nutt and her daughters taught both public and private school, she acted as postmistress, and her family donated land for the Community House. The local chapter of the Daughters of the Confederacy was named in her honor.

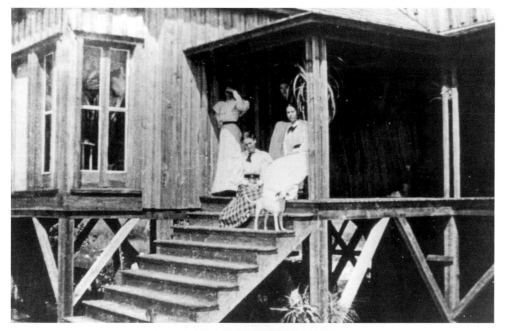

The Gables with the Nutt family, circa 1890. (Courtesy Historical Museum of Southern Florida)

Cordie and Lettie Nutt.

"Miss Cordie [Nutt] . . . would have us all come, sit around you know, and then she would begin to spin the fairy tales. And she just made them up . . . oh they were just marvelous, they were absolutely stupendous, marvelous."

Flora Sanibel Woodring Morris
1972 Interview

Jean Barnes holds her grandson George, who was born and died in 1893. The Barneses' church, Church of the Four Gospels, was built in the baby's memory and he was buried in a graveyard beside the church. Later his grandmother was also buried there. (Courtesy Jean Brock)

A gathering at the lighthouse dock before the turn of the century, perhaps for a momentous arrival or departure. Many are formally dressed. The intentness of these onlookers brings to mind one of the few Calusa phrases to be preserved: "Se-la-te-ga." It means "run to the lookout and see who is approaching," which seems to echo in this picture and on the island over the years.

Left: A palm-decorated steamer and barge provided a gala atmosphere for the Barnes party. The family seemed to have a flair for exuberance and drama. The father traveled worldwide on evangelistic tours accompanied by his daughter Marie who played on a portable organ and sang accompaniment. He never collected an offering when he preached, although donations were accepted. A graduate of Princeton Theological Seminary, he later was tried for heresy and left the church. On Sanibel the Barnes family opened The Sisters, a hotel later renamed Casa Ybel, then built a church and Thistle Lodge. These were elaborate beyond any other island structures, and Sunday promenades were held there on their Grand Boulevard. Members of the family said the hotel was opened in self-defense because of the Reverend's many visitors from all over the world. Myers, Florida, was the official post office for Fort Myers from 1876 to 1901, when the name reverted to Fort Myers.

(4—404.)

THE UNITED STATES OF AMERICA,

To all to whom these presents shall come, Greeting:

Homestead Certificate No. *11786*

APPLICATION *19288*

Whereas There has been deposited in the General Land Office of the United States a Certificate of the Register of the Land Office at *Gainesville, Florida*, whereby it appears that, pursuant to the Act of Congress approved 20th May, 1862, "To secure Homesteads to actual Settlers on the Public Domain," and the acts supplemental thereto, the claim of *Laetitia A. Nutt* has been established and duly consummated, in conformity to law, for the *Lot numbered five and the East half of the South West quarter of Section twenty-seven in Township forty-six South of Range twenty-five East of Tallahassee Meridian in Florida containing one hundred and fifty-nine acres and forty hundredths of an acre*

according to the Official Plat of the survey of the said Land, returned to the General Land Office by the Surveyor General:

Now know ye, That there is, therefore, granted by the **United States** unto the said *Laetitia A. Nutt* the tract of Land above described: TO HAVE AND TO HOLD the said tract of Land, with the appurtenances thereof, unto the said *Laetitia A. Nutt* and to *her* heirs and assigns forever.

In testimony whereof, I, *Grover Cleveland*, President of the United States of America, have caused these letters to be made Patent, and the Seal of the General Land Office to be hereunto affixed.

Given under my hand, at the City of Washington, the *fifth* day of *November*, in the year of our Lord one thousand eight hundred and *ninety five*, and of the Independence of the United States the one hundred and *twentieth.*

BY THE PRESIDENT: *Grover Cleveland*

By *M. McKean*, Secretary.

L. Q. C. Lamar, Recorder of the General Land Office.

Recorded, Vol. *24*, Page *186*

Homestead certificate recognizing Laetitia Nutt's claim, signed by President Grover Cleveland. When the island opened to homesteading, the east end was reserved for use by the government—the "lighthouse reservation." An 1876 map shows that Bowditch Point on the north end of Estero Island was considered part of this lighthouse reservation, keeping it public land as it is today. Perhaps beacons were considered for each side of the entrance to San Carlos Bay. (Courtesy Florence Young)

Chapter Three

The homesteading era had passed, but there was plenty of land to be purchased. In August 1896 these three ads appeared in the *Fort Myers Press*:

"FORTY ACRES of splendid vegetable land on Sanible [sic] Island, near steamboat landing, daily steamers, good location, a splendid bargain at $15 per acre. Suitable for early vegetables of all kinds."

Great Expectations

(1895–1910)

"80 acres on Sanibel Island, three acres facing the Gulf beach. A rare place for a winter residence or truck farm. Number one land, high and dry. Good school and church in ten minutes walk—A sanitarium for the ailing and a home for the healthy. Sanibel Island shipped over 10,000 boxes of tomatoes this season, averaging over $200 [yield] per acre."

"20-acres on Sanibell [sic] Island, half mile from shipping dock, schoolhouse on adjoining land. All prairie land, well-drained, and first-class vegetable land. Half a mile from a general store—"

Taken together, these ads tell much of the island's story for the period. Homesteaders generally acquired 160 acre properties—one-quarter of a section. After receiving land title, they began selling off acreage which they were not able to farm, often subdividing in logical halves, quarters, etc. Selling points of school, church, store, steamers, vegetables and their economic return, dry prairie, health conditions—all emphasized islander concerns and achievements at the turn of the century.

In 1894 Sanibel's population was 120 with 100 acres in truck [farming], two years later, due to post-freeze migration, the population was 350 with 500 acres in truck. It was estimated that ten acres were as much as one man could tend, and land sold for $10–$25 per acre. Laetitia Nutt's tax bill (state and county) for 1897 was $4.66 for 109 acres, on the Gulf. Homesteaders were joined by others including Geraty, Mackie, McIntyre, Bailey, Chapman, Rutland, Morris, Gibson, Holloway, Dinkens, Doane, Jenny, Riddle and Johnson.

Islanders settled in, and were concerned about schooling for their children. Disagreements arose with the Lee County Board of Public Instruction about the school site, delaying construction, but "a small but very attractive school" was operating by 1892. In 1894 it was blown down and a bid for a new school was awarded to E. T. Pell for $43. He also provided land for the schoolhouse. Controversy continued about the school site, several places being proposed and rejected by one side or the other. In 1896 the Board decided to send Sanibel's building allotment to Little Marco since no agreement could be reached. A month later F. M. Parks was paid $539 to build a schoolhouse on donated land. This is the building which after nearly seventy years became a community theater, the Pirate Playhouse.

Private schools advertised, like the Sanibel Home School operated in 1895-1896 by Mrs. L. A. Nutt. Circuit preachers like George Gatewood visited the island when they could and met in the schoolhouse or private homes. Resident preachers including George Fitzhugh and George Barnes filled in. Reverend Barnes built a church seating 300, the Church of the Four Gospels, on his property.

The post office was established at Sanibel in 1894 and another in 1897 at the community of Wulfert. Stores and packing houses appeared. Economic concerns were balanced by entertainments—plays, shelling contests, horse races, ball games. Island residents were described as cosmopolitan. Winter visitors brought new ideas, diversions and points of view.

Archaeologist Frank Hamilton Cushing stopped at numerous mounds in Charlotte Harbor and visited Sanibel. Other noted people frequented the two hotels, The Sisters and The Matthews, where accommodations were simple but well presented. Enjoyment of the natural world was overriding. At The Sisters the hotel guests sometimes manned a seine net on the beach. The *Fort Myers Press* reported "seine fishing is currently the most fashionable amusement on the island. Ladies enjoy the fun even more than the men." On one occasion a guest stationed in deeper water refused to bring his portion of the net to the beach. When others approached him to explain what he should be going, the problem was revealed. He had lost his bathing suit—he claimed, to a large shark!

The Spanish-American War alerted the islands. News of the explosion of the *Maine* and its aftermath made islanders realize how vulnerable Sanibel was. Cattle and commerce had always flowed south, but would war and suffering flow north? George Schultz, telegraph operator at Punta Rassa, was sanguine. He declared the little brass cannon which he fired off to celebrate New Year's Eve and July Fourth would be used if any attack on the Bay seemed imminent.

But the war ended, and tourism flourished. Hunting, tarpon fishing, cruising the endless waterways of southwest Florida, attracted more visitors every year. A trio of fishermen trolling near the lighthouse waded ashore to request something cold to drink one afternoon, to discover a trash fire burning out of control. The Shanahans were beating out the flames. The men grabbed some palm fronds and helped extinguish the fire. Mrs. Shanahan rewarded them with fresh-made lemonade. The men were Thomas Edison, Harvey Firestone, and Henry Ford.

Rural Free Delivery began on Sanibel on April 2, 1900, one of the nation's early routes. The National Grange, a farmers organization, was active in getting Congress to provide free rural delivery of mail, and our farming community was an early beneficiary. It seems anachronistic that a century later our sister island of Captiva still has no mail delivery.

Henry B. Plant's railroad line ended at Punta Gorda. He used steamers to extend his reach to the south end of Charlotte Harbor and Fort Myers. In 1904 the railroad finally arrived in Fort Myers.

Cuban fishing smacks sailed offshore catching fish for their market, although trade in dried or salted fish had faded away. Most fishing ranchos, which were based on-shore, had ended operation by the turn of the century. As Americans settled the islands mutterings had increased about the "Spanish fishermen [who] . . . take millions of our fish and give no return." The railhead in Punta Gorda and ice plants (which produced electricity as a by-product) meant the era of iced fish shipped by boxcar had begun, and the money and fish remained American. Interest in shipping dried or salted fish declined.

Fishing guides offered their services to winter visitors and often developed a following. In 1908 the Clubhouse was built by a group of fishermen so they could be near their guide, Sam Woodring.

In October of 1910 the islands were surprised by a major late-season hurricane, the worst since 1873. It tore green citrus from the trees and flung them around like cannonshot, truck farmers lost their crops, and houses, docks and packing warehouses were destroyed. Eighty percent of the fruit crop was lost. What had seemed a charmed place showed another aspect.

Mrs. Irene Shanahan, wife of the lighthouse keeper, and her turkeys.

This Casa Ybel group is displaying a variety of game including several turkeys, perhaps from a turkey shoot. In the center are two dressed-out deer, to the left a rabbit, and right a gator belly-skin. (Courtesy Jean Brock)

"Our Sanibel Island conveyance" before the turn of the century in front of Matthews Wharf. (Courtesy Historical Museum of Southern Florida)

"I heard him [grandfather Jimmy Riddle] tell about when the seines would make a catch out there [Clam Bayou], he'd take his mule, and go over there and help to pull the net with the mule."

John Peurifoy
1979 Interview

The Bailey home continues to stand on Periwinkle at Donax. The original section was built in 1896 for $530. It is still owned by the family.

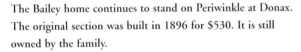

Many farmers were attracted to Sanibel after Florida's momentous double freeze of 1894–1895. James Riddle and his son George came to Sanibel in 1895. James is flanked by several of George's children. Back row: Louise (Waldron), James's wife Jeannie Florrie, Irene (Adkins). Front row: Jeannie Clyde (Crumpler), Blanche (Rhode), Marion, Jim, and George. Florrie (Woodring) missed the picture.

"One of the first jobs that Daddy had was hauling watermelons . . . he loaded the wagon with watermelons and walked along the side of it . . . he said he didn't ride because he could pile more watermelons on. . . . so he made the best loads."

Francis Bailey
1973 Interview

Charlotta Matthews with Nellie, the horse. Will and Hallie Matthews, Charlotta's parents, came to Sanibel from Kentucky after hearing about it from Reverend Barnes. They soon began to provide rooms and dining facilities for winter visitors, becoming known as The Matthews. Eventually the Matthews family gave Gulf lots to visitors who promised to build on them and take their meals with them. In 1937 the name was changed to Island Inn, and in 1957 it was sold by the family to a group of long-time guests, forming the Island Inn Corporation.

Nancy Pearson, a teacher, with several children including Russell Buck whose hand she holds. The Buck family's Buttonwood Cottage was east of The Matthews. In his teens Russell Buck attended The Snyder Outdoor School for Boys, whose winter home was on Captiva.

Captain A. R. Robinson built his home west of The Matthews in 1910, taking advantage of the offer by the Matthews family of a lot if he would build on it and take meals at the Inn. The house still exists, having been moved about a mile to the east, and is now owned by Mr. and Mrs. Sam Bailey.

Revenue cutter *McLain,* a sidewheel steamer, patrolled Charlotte Harbor under the command of Captain Hand. The 1898 Spanish-American War made islanders wonder if the war would come to them. A detachment of the U.S. Signal Corps took over lighthouse operations and erected observation towers along the shore. Tampa Bay to the north was a major staging area for troops enroute to Cuba. The telegraph station at Punta Rassa was the first recipient nationally of the news of the sinking of the battleship *Maine* on February 15, which precipitated the conflict. (Courtesy Historical Museum of Southern Florida)

The Gibson family at their tomato packing house near Wulfert. The family came in 1900, first working for the farm partners Dwight and Holloway.

"I got off the bulkhead down there at Wulfert where my folks lived, and the next morning I packed up my other pair of britches and shirt, and went down there and met the *Gladys. . . ."* [on being hired by the Kinzie Line]

Arthur Gibson
1968 Interview

John B. and Lucy Daniels with children Bertha and Haskell (on father's knee) about 1900 on Sanibel. In the 1926 storm Haskell Daniels and his wife were staying near Matthews Wharf on the bay in the building which became Miss Charlotta's Tea Room. During the eye of the storm, they attempted to go to the lighthouse by car to send a telegram to Frank Bailey to notify him that his store had been destroyed. The car was overwhelmed by storm waves, and the Daniels couple had to wade to safety. Mrs. Daniels was pregnant at the time. The wrecked car remained on the beach for years as a marker of the storm.

The *H. B. Plant* (the second of the same name) was brought to Charlotte Harbor waters
to replace the plucky little *Alice Howard* on the Punta Gorda-Fort Myers run a year after
it was built in 1899. Henry Plant had died before seeing his namesake vessel afloat.
(Courtesy Historical Museum of Southern Florida)

Thomas A. Edison on the porch of Casa Ybel. Edison visited the islands in search of tropical plants for experimentation. He was interested in fibers and natural rubber, among other projects. Mina Edison enjoyed shelling, and in the 1920s had Clarence Rutland deliver several bags of shells to her.

Thistle Lodge at Casa Ybel was built by Mr. Edward M. Duncan when he and Georgia Barnes married. Miss Barnes, the daughter of the Reverend George and Jean Barnes, had homesteaded on Sanibel along with her sister, brother, and parents. In November 1896 the *Fort Myers Press* indicated the Hon. E. M. Duncan's "palatial residence on the Grand Boulevard is nearing completion." It described the Grand Boulevard on Sunday afternoons as a parade ground with "handsome turnouts, spirited horses, and beautiful ladies." (Courtesy Historical Museum of Southern Florida)

"On Easter Sunday the ladies dressed in their full finery—long skirts reaching the ground—full length sleeves and with those hot 'neckchokers'—huge hats decorated with sea shells, sea grasses, urchins and other things washed on the beach." (Courtesy Hal Tayntor)

The elegant Church of the Four Gospels stood on the Gulf shore, its top-mounted cross meant to attract passing sailors. This memorial to Reverend Barnes' dead grandson seated 300 and was erected through Miss (Marie) Barnes' efforts. The Reverend George Barnes preached at the church when on-island. It was demolished in the 1910 hurricane, although some of its pews were salvaged and placed in Sanibel's Community Church when it was built in 1917. (Courtesy Jean Brock)

Overall view of The Sisters, or Casa Ybel, prior to 1900. Visible is the Church of the Four Gospels, far left, Thistle Lodge, cottages, and a windmill. In addition to the improvements made on their property, in May 1897 George O. Barnes, his son William and son-in-law Edward Duncan incorporated the Sanibel Island Railway & Construction Company. What they had in mind is not now known. (Courtesy Jean Brock)

The *St. Lucie* in 1903. She began running the Punta Gorda-Fort Myers route in 1896 with the *Alice Howard*. The Atlantic Coast Line had purchased the Plant System's assets after Plant's death in 1899, but the railroad did not extend into Fort Myers until 1904, so steamers continued to be the transport of choice. (Courtesy Historical Museum of Southern Florida)

Lewis and Jennie Doane in their Wulfert garden, January 1904. Jennie was Wulfert's postmistress, and an independent woman for the time. The high fencing may have been to discourage deer.

The Holloway house in 1905 at Wulfert. Wulfert with close to one hundred residents was an "up and coming" community in the early years of the century, with its own school, post office, store, dock, and bulkhead for shipment of crops. Jennie Doane is at right foreground and Captain Duffy is the short bearded man near center. Duffy Creek in the refuge carries his name.

Lewis Doane collecting mailbags from the Wulfert docks in the early 1900s. The Wulfert post office was established in February 1897 and was discontinued in July of 1935. The reason for Wulfert's name remains a mystery. It was said to be chosen by a postal inspector when the Doanes and the Dwights, another Wulfert family, each wanted the post office named after themselves. Perhaps it was a family name as Washington Irving, the creator of Rip van Winkle, used the Dutch first name Wolfert in some of his stories.

Wulfert school was south of the landing near today's intersection of Wildlife Drive and Wulfert Road. This little building held eighteen students in 1902, and operated until 1924, occasionally combining with Captiva to have enough students. Wulfert celebrated Thanksgiving in 1903 with a "dinner in a shady grove on the banks of Bowie [Bowen's] Bayou" and a program at the school. (Courtesy Southwest Florida Historical Society)

Cuban fishing smacks in the harbor, San Carlos Bay.

"The rough water [from storms] would kill the fish so bad in the well, they [the Cuban fishing smacks] would sail down and get in the lee of Sanibel. Sometimes they wouldn't go inside [San Carlos Bay]. They would anchor between Casa Ybel and the lighthouse. You see, that runs east and west down there . . ."

Belton Johnson
1982 Interview

Left: A waterspout seaward of the lighthouse. Waterspouts may be seen a number of times each summer near Sanibel. In the 1930s Captain Leon Crumpler was caught up in one waterspout on the ferry while crossing the bay. Lighthouse keeper Roscoe McLane complimented him on his seamanship—saying it was "pretty smart" the way Crumpler turned around and went south. Crumpler agreed without telling him the spout had turned the ferry around and he'd come close to losing the boat.

"[On the ferry caught in a waterspout] raining so hard it couldn't run off. . . . All at once it was calm. Perfectly calm. . . . you couldn't see out, there was a circle right straight around you . . . you had difficulty in breathing. . . . it seemed like the water was coming down in the middle and going up on the outside."

Leon Crumpler
1968 Interview

Tarpon hunting became so intense that a "floating hotel" for fishermen was anchored at Boca Grande in 1902 when this photo was taken. The Hughes [or "Hews scow"] which accommodated ten or twelve fishermen was moved to Captiva Pass another year, and then San Carlos Bay, where it was brought on-shore and turned into the Sanibel House at Reed's Landing by Lucy Reed Richardson. John Roach was induced in build the Useppa Inn in 1902 for twenty fishing guests when tarpon fishing at Captiva Pass outgrew the "scow." (Courtesy Historical Museum of Southern Florida)

Sam Woodring weighs in an impressive tarpon at Useppa. Edward vom Hofe, with the handlebar moustache, developed fishing tackle. While fishing from the "floating hotel" in Captiva Pass, he caught a 210-pound tarpon, the record for many years. The struggle using his leather thumb brake reel was so "desperate" that he invented his automatic handle drag reel, an ingenious design that is now used on all large fishing reels. His reels are collector's items today. Tarpon fishing at the turn of the century involved rowing the client to the fishing grounds—usually Boca Grande or Captiva Pass—in sixteen-or-eighteen foot boats. Later a steamer towed a string of rowboats to the grounds, until gasoline engines took over. (Courtesy Ralph Woodring)

The *Gladys* of the Kinzie Brothers Steamer Line was a well-known steamer which maintained her tie to Sanibel from 1902 until she sank in 1936. The Kinzies had rebuilt the *Gladys*, doubling her length while leaving her width the same. After renovation she was seventy-eight feet long, and burned a cord of wood a day. Wood for the steamers was largely cut from the Caloosahatchee's north shore, now Cape Coral. When the *Gladys* sank she was still on duty. The ferry had been docking at the Sanibel Packing Co., but that trip took an additional fifteen minutes and a sand flat caused trouble at low tide, so the Kinzies were building a new ferry slip at the east end of the island. The *Gladys*, loaded with lumber and anchored offshore for several days while work continued, sank in twenty-five feet of water one night. Declared a navigational hazard, she was hauled ashore and burned.

". . . tourists would go over to Sanibel and Captiva in the winter, there were hotels over there . . . They rebuilt [the steamer *Gladys*] and extended it out about forty feet to use on the island run . . . The *Gladys* was very long and narrow, . . . a good running boat and was very reasonable to operate . . ."

Ernest Kinzie
1989 Interview

"Mail time was a big event then. All the cottagers would congregate in front of the main eating hall. The mail would arrive in a one-horse buggy and Miss Marie Barnes would call out the names of the lucky ones." [Hal Tayntor] Sanibel was one of the first post offices in the United States to have Rural Free Delivery.

The Sisters' dining room was well-appointed, but guests had a good time. One of the Barnes grandchildren spotted a visitor combing his moustache with the tines of a fork. The cloth napery, crystal, and centerpiece of roses is complemented by decorations of native finds. (Courtesy Jean Brock)

Hal Tayntor and his pet gopher tortoise on a Casa Ybel cottage porch. He related, "Sanibel then was wonderful. Today it's quite different!!!"

Charles Tayntor, about thirteen, with an alligator he shot. Tayntor's father was an expert revolver shot and a member of the U.S. Olympic Shooting Team. He spent much of his Sanibel time target-practicing, and often was called upon to dispatch sharks and devil fish [manta rays] brought up on the beach.

Isabel Sears secures her hat against the Gulf breeze. On an 1895 trip the Sears family stayed aboard their houseboat near Tarpon Bay. When they awoke the next morning the water all around was covered with melted butter. They had "put it over the side to keep it cool, but it didn't get cool." Like many other visitors, several generations of the Sears family have settled here.

The *Free Lance*, a wooden propeller vessel built in 1906 in Fort Myers, coming into Sanibel. The *Free Lance* was nearly seventy-eight feet long and fifteen feet wide, fifty-one gross tons and had a four-man crew. She was registered at Key West, the nearest place to register a boat at that time, and carried a passenger license.

Traveling across the island to Casa Ybel in 1908. Alice Tayntor, far right. The drive was leisurely. A 1904 Casa Ybel brochure says, "At Matthews wharf [end of Bailey Road near the causeway] the hotel wagonette meets [you], and a forty minutes drive transfers [you] from the bay to the Gulf shore . . ."

The *Pastime* was a sternwheeler built in Jacksonville in 1904 suited to the shallow estuaries of Charlotte Harbor. Only eleven feet wide, it was fifty-seven feet long, twenty-two tons gross weight. With its cargo of crates and roof-top chairs for passengers, the *Pastime* has the appearance of the excursion mailboat which ran to the islands from 1936 to 1964.

Cuban fishing smacks, some as long as 125 feet, fished the Sanibel off-shore waters. The fishing trips could last several weeks. The sail-powered vessels stored live fish within their holds, which were essentially huge live-wells, and the crew lived on deck. They slept in hammocks, cooked on-board, and when storms threatened sometimes found shelter in San Carlos Bay or in the lee of Sanibel's southern shore in winter.

[The Cuban fishermen and their sailing smacks] "knew that bad weather was coming so they come on inside and anchored down here at off the lighthouse, about where the old ferry landing was. . . ."

Jake Stokes
1982 Interview

John Morris and Etta Shehee Morris in the front yard of their Sanibel farmhouse. Married in 1904, Etta died two years later. John later married Flora Woodring and they moved to Fort Myers.

Commercial fishermen hauling nets off Captiva in 1907. These were probably stop nets which were laid at high tide to block a channel, catching all fish passing through as the tide went low. The boats would be filled and then towed to a fish house for weighing and storage on ice. Every other day a runboat stopped to drop off ice and hauled the fish to the rail connection in Punta Gorda. (Courtesy Historical Museum of Southern Florida)

Gathering oysters for a roast? Fiddler crabs for bait? The Sanibel stoop is a century old and more.

[The net fishermen] "pulled all of it together and pulled the fish into the boat, they didn't have to pick 'em out, they poured them into the boat."

Clarence Rutland
1979 Interview

You get thirsty after a day on the water. The long pier at Tarpon Bay was a frequent starting point for island exploring.

Below: Boating and bathing by the Casa Ybel pier, which was gradually extended over the years. Gulfside piers have disappeared over the years because of hurricanes and winter northers. Piers have existed at Island Inn, Casa Ybel, Shell Basket, the Lighthouse (Gulf and bay), the Dixie Dock, Ocean Leather Company dock, Bailey Road, Reed's Landing, Wulfert, as well as the ferry landing.

The Tayntor family enjoy the pier.

Right: Manta ray caught between the pilings of the Casa Ybel dock. "One time one [of] these huge sea monsters became entangled in the bulkhead of the long pier we had then. A Mr. Duncan hung him up—13 feet long and 17 feet wide . . ." [Hal Tayntor] Edward Duncan operated Casa Ybel with his brother-in-law William Barnes. Although large and fearsome-looking, the manta ray is a plankton feeder and not a threat to man.

Casa Ybel, 1910. "Mother [Mary Hutchins Tayntor] is ready for a walk on the beach, with her shell basket. Our cottage is in the background." Hal Tayntor commented that "she was protected from the sun from head to feet—no one was interested in getting a tan then but avoiding one. But shells—they were glorious . . ."

The Sanibel Tomato Pickers were 1910 Caloosa Valley Baseball champs. Their tomatoes were considered top-notch in markets as distant as New York. Front: Sam Woodring, Joe Dowd, unknown, and Pete Jenny. Back: Ed Hughes, unknown, Frank Padgett, Will Reed, Steele Doyle, and John Morris.

Elise Lilley Fuller was only eight years old when the 1910 storm hit Sanibel. The Lilley family had come from their Fort Myers home to their Sanibel farmhouse, shown here the day after the storm. The hurricane tore off the porches and water surged around the house. Her father used interior doors to batten down the windows during the blow, moving them to the other side of the house when the wind changed direction after the eye passed. Mamie, their mule, remained in her stall in knee-deep water as the barn collapsed around her. Once the storm subsided, they hitched Mamie to a cart and went to the lighthouse along the beach. The river had broken through the dune so they had to force Mamie into the waves to cross on a sandbar. In the photo foreground are crop remains, to the right the wrecked barn, in front of the house Mamie (?) and the beach. Elise considered the storm a great adventure. Mamie's opinion is unknown.

"In the eye of the storm [1910] it was very quiet, and the rain wasn't coming down so hard. We opened the front door and looked carefully out. The front porch was gone. . . . The Gulf was up under the floor boards of the house. . . . We could count four porpoises swimming around the house."

Elise Fuller
1978 Interview

The *Success* prepares to load passengers and freight in 1912. Freight on a package up to fifty pounds was ten cents.

"Everything came there [Reed Dock], all the freight, the *Success*, and all those boats. . . . my father besides being the postmaster, he was the census-taker, and he was an express agent, and all the vegetables [he would label the crates for shipping]."

Carrie Reed Ebsworth
1992 Interview

Chapter Four

The hurricane of 1910 was powerful, damaging the citrus crop by stripping the trees of the season's fruit. But it was a wet storm with much rain, which washed the wind-deposited salt from the soil, so planting could continue for the truck farmers.

The Church of the Four Gospels was destroyed, but church services continued in the schoolhouse. By spring, Mrs. Buck was raising money for an organ. In a special service at the school Bishop Crane confirmed Harry Bailey and Flora

Sun and Storms

(1911–1928)

Parker, and by the end of the decade a new Community Church and a Baptist Church had been erected.

Other events included the third annual Shell Show at Casa Ybel, a tradition which started there in 1909. The Bailey boys held a "Bachelor's Ball" at Matthews Wharf. Political organization and improvements expanded. Businesses prospered. J. H. Johnson opened a blacksmith and wheelwright shop. In 1911 the Lee County Ferry across Blind Pass was operated by farmer John Boring. The ferry was a lighter, or motorized barge, a type of boat used for fishing, phosphate and shell mining, and houseboats. In 1912 the Sanibel Association met at The Gables. In 1913 Sanibel was declared a state bird reservation, a phone system connected several homes and businesses on-island and Webb Shanahan began delivering mail in a new Ford instead of by horse, a first for the county.

As the decade continued, the county dredged channels at Wulfert and through Blind Pass, replacing inconvenient bulkheads offshore and allowing steamers to dock directly at the island. Nearly a dozen pianos graced the island. The *Dixie*, a new steamer the Kinzie Brothers had ordered built in New York, was put into service, and shell mining of Indian mounds to pave Fort Myers roads accelerated. The *Dixie* was often booked for church trips to Sanibel and moonlight river excursions. In 1915 a canning company was built at Tarpon Bay. By 1918, Boring's ferry was replaced by Blind Pass's first bridge. Some of the island's early settlers were being replaced as well. James Ashmore, Henry Shanahan, and Laetitia Nutt died and others moved away.

The winter tourist season continued to attract the rich and famous, including the Astors, Vanderbilts, and President Teddy Roosevelt. The Snyder School of Captiva, which from 1913 to 1926 taught outdoor skills along with the classics to its boys, developed ties with numerous islanders. Like the farmers, commercial fishermen harvested their riches. In 1921 the Ocean Leather Company began processing sharks and other large sea-creatures near the lighthouse, one of their several Florida locations. The state continued to use convicts for roadwork on Sanibel.

Sanibel was not immune to the boom era of the 1920s. Speculators liked what they saw of the island. Development companies bought land and sold shares. In 1925 H. H. Ford purchased Silver Key for $100,000, a purchase he probably regretted. In 1993 when the City of Sanibel purchased the key they paid less than half of that when figured in 1925 dollars. The first Sanibel Ferry, in 1926, was an adjunct to Sanibel developments called Suniland Beach and Lantana del Mar. The ferry disappeared in the 1926 hurricane, as did development plans, investors' money and the Florida boom.

For Sanibel as for most of Florida, the 1926 hurricane was a final blow to an already faltering prosperity. Sanibel farmers relied on water transportation to take crops to the railroad and market. But in 1924 the railroad had expanded south of Fort Myers, and opened large farmable areas to easy rail access. The Sanibel advantage was gone. To get island crops to market was now more expensive than for competitors' crops. When the hurricane left fields saturated with salt many farmers moved to town or started farming on the mainland. The storm which devastated Lake Okeechobee two years later blew across a changed island.

Charles Henry Williams, Sanibel Lighthouse keeper from 1910 to 1923, later went to Gasparilla Island, retiring in 1932. Keeping the light operating to a precise schedule no matter what the weather conditions is an exacting task, and Henry's hobby reflected that influence. He relaxed by repairing clocks and watches. (Courtesy Gladys Williams Hill)

Hattie, son Martin, and Henry Williams. Daughter Gladys, born at the Sanibel Light, remembers dashing up and down the stairway to the tower before the family left Sanibel when she was seven. (Courtesy Gladys Williams Hill)

William Doyle with daughter Myra about 1911. Doyle and Will Geraty sold their store to the Bailey Brothers in 1899, and the same year each married a Cooper girl, possibly in a double wedding. Geraty made the comment that Sanibel mosquitoes were "big enough to carry a large iron washpot several miles."

The Clubhouse on Woodring Point. A number of Cincinnati businessmen built the clubhouse in 1908 to be close to their fishing guide Sam Woodring. The McCullough family purchased shares from the other partners and continues to live there today. Shortly after being built it became a hurricane refuge for some of the Woodring family during the 1910 storm.

Fishing from the Clubhouse—Albert McCullough, unknown, Huber Lloyd, George Underhill and Sam Woodring. George Underhill was a guide and friend of the Woodrings. His mother, Safia, married Sam Ellis in the Woodring home Christmas Day, 1888, and the family lived on the south shore of Tarpon Bay.

Below: The Sanibel House at Reed's Landing about 1911, owned by Lucy Reed Daniels. Two cisterns on the left collected rainwater, the water supply, from the roof. The children are J. B. Daniels, Hazel Reed, Carrie Reed, and Haskell Daniels. To the right of the hotel is Captain William H. Reed's two-story house, next is Postmaster William S. Reed's home.

Sanibel school in 1911. The children are sitting in the road. Later changes to the building included a second room, additional windows, and lowered roofline. The bell and belfry disappeared, possibly in the 1926 storm.

The Willis home was referred to as the Hurricane House after it was blown off its pilings in the 1926 storm. It was built before 1900. (Courtesy Sanibel Public Library)

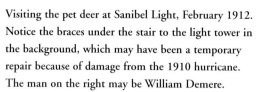

Visiting the pet deer at Sanibel Light, February 1912. Notice the braces under the stair to the light tower in the background, which may have been a temporary repair because of damage from the 1910 hurricane. The man on the right may be William Demere.

"I heard Grandpa [Silver Key homesteader Jimmy Riddle] talk about there was deer on the island. That's how come they called it Buck Key."

John Peurifoy
1979 Interview

Inside a packing house, 1911. In the 1920s, Clarence Rutland earned seven cents per crate packing tomatoes and peppers for farmers W. D. Swint, Robert Mitchell, and S. J. Turner. Rutland made deliveries, did road work, and farmed, among other jobs. He kept a memo book recording the date and job, sending bills and noting payments. Packing tended to occur in January and February, although tomatoes were shipped as late as April when they had to be replanted because of freeze damage. Rutland recorded numbers of crates he packed in a day from a few to eighty or more.

A Sanibel tomato field.

[Bailey's General Store] "on the dock over the bay . . . until the hurricane of '26 came through and . . . blew it over in the bay. . . . we went back down there and there they were, the building is gone and the dock is out there and they were diving trying to find the safe. They did find it. And, then of course they rebuilt."

Jacob Johnson
1994 Interview

Above: Matthews Wharf, and the Sanibel Packing Company store. A main shipping point on and off the island, the complex was destroyed in the 1926 hurricane, necessitating the "new" store being built on land.

The *Success* pulls away, her paddlewheel spinning. The *Success* was built in 1906 and burned a year later. In 1908 the Kinzies bought her at auction and put her on the Punta Gorda to Sanibel-Captiva route after they split her down the middle to widen her and add larger engines. She also towed barges of shell (dredged from Indian mounds at Shell Point) upriver to Fort Myers for road paving.

Left: An early photo of the Barracks at Island Inn. Work was begun on the twenty-two room, three-story building in the spring of 1915. Notice the pier to the right.

". . . we always kept a spider and a spider web . . . in the summer at each end of the hall upstairs [for mosquito control.]

Milbrey Rushworth
1992 Interview

In the living room at The Matthews, 1914.

Sunday school at the school, January 10, 1915. Included in the photograph are Mrs. J. S. Page; Mrs. Geo. Buck; Lyman Frank; S. E. Gapinski; Jesse, Katie, Oliver, and Estelle Adkins; Mrs. Emma and father Baxter Young; Mrs. Emmie and LeRoy Johnson; Ernest Bailey; Ed Waldron; Irene, Louise, George, Clyde, James, and Marion Riddle; Pearl Shannahan and two of her boys; Ed, Dora, and Alma Jenny; Clarence Rutland; Homer Wiles, Belton, Ray, and Fred Johnson; Jake and Hugh Fowler; Bertha, Haskell, and J. B. Daniels; Florence, Carrie, and Hazel Reed; Mr. Hughes; School Principal Otto Gorish. (Courtesy Sanibel Public Library)

Reed's Landing in 1914. Hotel, post office, and shipping dock on San Carlos Bay. The Kinzie steamer stopped here twice daily. (Courtesy Sanibel Public Library)

Hazel, Carrie, Leila and Florence, daughters of Postmaster William S. Reed, in 1915.

"they had good parties those days . . . they would go down to the lighthouse . . . those floors were hardwood polished floors, varnished, every room had a fireplace, . . . and we used to have picnics underneath of the lighthouse . . ."

Carrie Reed Ebsworth
1993 Interview

William S. Reed in front of the post office. For two months from December 1894 to February 1895 the post mark was Reed instead of Sanibel. Although the name didn't stick, Reed did. He remained postmaster until 1940, when his daughter Hazel Reed Godard took over.

William Kitchell built steamboats on the St. Johns River before coming to the islands in 1897. One of his boats, the *Clara*, preceded him to the west coast, and ran mail, freight, and passengers three times a week from Punta Gorda to Fort Myers, stopping at Sanibel, Punta Rassa, and St. James City. (Courtesy Frances Willis)

Kitchell's boatyard, possibly on his Woodring Point land bought from Anna Woodring in 1912. He also owned property on Captiva and other islands, including an island at Blind Pass.

Left: Theodore Roosevelt lived on this lighter, a motorized barge with cabin, when he visited Captiva to fish for sharks and devil rays. His associate, Russell Coles, from Danville, Virginia was interested in devil ray and shark fishing commercially, and hoped to interest the public in the creatures as food fish, but his plan never gained a following. In 1921 the Ocean Leather Company established a shark factory on Sanibel, processing leather and shark liver oil. They planned "to utilize everything about the sharks but their bite." Fishing pressure was intense, and sharks are slow to mature, so the creatures were quickly depopulated and the industry shut down.

Dock at Wulfert approximately 1914–1920. In 1914 the Lee County Commission appropriated money to channelize several places adjacent to Sanibel and Captiva to eliminate the need for bulkheads—buildings on pilings placed offshore beside deeper water. A channel five to six feet deep at low tide provided direct access to Wulfert for steamer service and eliminated the time-consuming transfers of mail, cargo, passengers and produce. It was noted that 10,000 crates of vegetables were shipped from the Wulfert bulkhead each season.

Bill Kimball, from the Snyder School, looking piratical. Kimball later became president of the Island Inn Corporation.

Hobbs, from the Snyder School, with his catch. The boys frequently visited "Old Man" Kessen, who farmed near Wulfert on an Indian Mound, and ran a museum displaying the curios he had collected. Gator hunting and mound digging were part of Kessen's attraction for the boys.

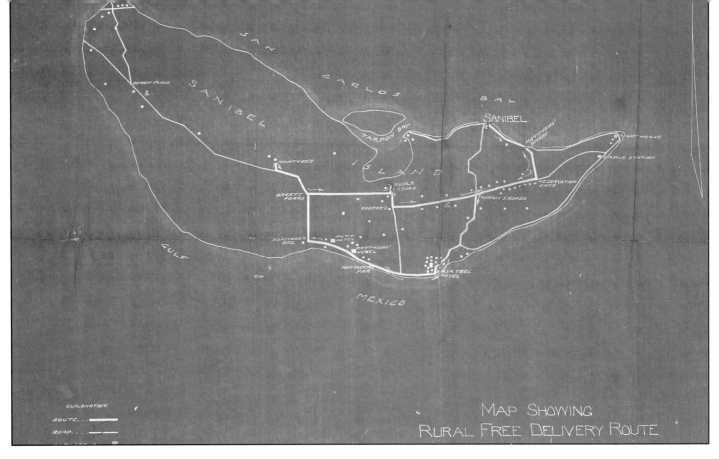

1905 Rural Free Delivery Route Map

In 1894 Kentuckian Ernest Royal Bailey was the first of the Baileys to come to Sanibel, and in 1898 he went on to Cuba to explore the possibility of farming there. In addition to Sanibel farmland and the packing company, Ernest invested in some farmland at Estero. He was active in drama and the arts, and his church. Something of a free spirit, he sunbathed "au naturel" each day.

Harry Bailey in his lime grove. Brother of Ernest and Frank, Harry later moved to Fort Myers.

Fresh Florida Grown Key Limes

MATURED ON TREES

$1.50 per carton containing about one hundred Limes according to size
delivered to you to you by express prepaid.

$2.50 for one quarter box about twice the size of carton prepaid by
express to you.

FLORIDA KEY LIMES ARE THE ORIGINAL LIMES AND HAVE
THEIR OWN DISTINCTIVE FLAVOR

(Buy American Grown Products)

SANIBEL PACKING COMPANY

Sanibel, Florida

Key Limes, prices.

E R BAILEY   FRANK P BAILEY

Sanibel Packing Company

GROWERS & SHIPPERS OF
FRUITS AND VEGETABLES

LIMES AND TOMATOES OUR SPECIALTIES

SANIBEL FLORIDA

Business card for Sanibel Packing Company.

A family photo on Frank and Annie Meade Matthews Bailey's wedding day, June 6, 1919,
at the Matthews Hotel, just before the couple, in traveling clothes, left on their honey-
moon. (Left to right): Reverend Shore, Harry and Miriam Bailey, Ernest Bailey, bride and
groom Frank and Annie Bailey, Hallie and Will Matthews, Charlotta Matthews, Alice
Bailey Garvey and husband Will.

Isabel Terrill and Grace Hemingway stand in the shadow of a plane traveling from New York to Cuba, which landed near the Barracks at the Matthews Hotel in 1921. Hemingway was the mother of writer Ernest Hemingway.

Bailey Buck motors along Woodring Point in his Oldsmobile. The boy on the porch is presumably aiming at something in the prickly-pear cactus, right.

Interior of the Buttonwood Cottage belonging to the Bailey Buck family in the 1920s. Son Russell Buck often came home on winter weekends from the Snyder School on Captiva, and the Matthews Hotel next door to Buttonwood Cottage was a popular destination for the schoolboys for parties. The cottage still exists although it was moved in the 1970s.

[1921 hurricane at Gray Gables] ". . . all downstairs was the kitchen . . . woodburning stoves . . . and then that storm just floated all the food down over the floor . . . my dad went down, and swum around, and he got some grits, and cans . . . some canned beef . . . and so we ate."

Oscar Gavin
1980 Interview

The Gables in 1921 with twin stairs and enclosed below. By 1925 The Gables was owned by the Convent of the Transfiguration, and in 1960 was repurchased by members of the family. (Courtesy Elinore Dormer)

A 32-foot-long "blue, sulphur bottomed whale" near the Ocean Leather Company in 1926. Clarence Rutland is in the center. Evidently the whale was not processed as it was towed into the Gulf some days later. The "shark factory" processed shark skins into leather, livers into oil, and fins were sent to Honolulu "for the Chinese"—1200 pounds of shark fins in one 1921 shipment. Meat and intestines became fertilizer and soap, and cartilage was turned into glue. The company had locations in the Keys and the Florida west coast as well as Sanibel. Shark hides were salted and shipped to a New Jersey tannery near the company's main office in New York. Many of the creatures were netted—one assumes with heavy rope netting. The president of the company, Dr. Alfred Ehrenreich, lived on Sanibel with his family.

Harry Walker and Charlie Minyard, 1920s. The Walker family came to Sanibel in the 1920s to settle and farm. Five generations of the family have continued to be islanders to the present.

The Sawyer Cottage in February 1924, rented for the season by the Mayer family. Pictured is Daisy Mayer, Elinore Mayer, Jane Rider, and Emma Lefrese. (Courtesy Elinore Dormer)

The class of 1924. With the advent of vehicular traffic, the schoolyard was fenced. Back row, second from left is Annie Laurie Mitchell, and her brother William Robert is in front of her in dark shorts. (Courtesy Anne Daves)

Young Robert Mitchell feeds the family chickens in the side yard. The front door is screened, the side porch sports mosquito switches by the door. Robert remembered his father burning smudge pots using old fertilizer sacks to keep mosquitoes down in summer. The Mitchell farm was in approximately the same area as the earlier Morris farm, and this may be the same farmhouse. (Courtesy Anne Daves)

Hallie Matthews is flanked by Haskell Daniels (left) and Ron McCoy in 1925 next to the Matthews Hotel. McCoy still remembers Hallie as "a very gracious lady." He stayed at the Matthews and worked for his uncle, Dr. Harry Opre, who was developing some property on Island Inn Road. McCoy later worked for Frank Bailey at the store, then at the lighthouse doing maintenance. McCoy described Haskell Daniels as Frank Bailey's right-hand man. (Courtesy Ron McCoy)

Clyde Riddle clowns around.

Right: Collecting and clowning on the beach. Sanibel's reputation as a shelling mecca has long been appreciated, and residents could make a few extra dollars scavenging the beach. The expanse of the island's treeless prairie is apparent behind Jerry Lauer in December 1925. (Courtesy Al and Joy Dobbs)

A turned loggerhead sea turtle became the platform for the Shanahan girls, Snookie and Lorraine, about 1926. Cousin Clarisse stands in the center. The loggerhead doubtless became a meal. Notice the axe at the extreme left. Turtle meat was used in steaks and turtle-burgers, and was considered similar to beef. At least one early restaurant's hamburgers were rumored to be loggerhead turtle meat. (Courtesy Al and Joy Dobbs)

"Henry's fish camp." Henry Shanahan, the lighthouse keeper's son, owned this "getaway" in Tarpon Bay. Nets are spread to dry on the right. (Courtesy Al and Joy Dobbs)

The Sanibel Ferry began running in early 1926, but was destroyed by the fall hurricane. Jerry Lauer (left) was engineer, and Gene Shanahan Captain. The ferry made three trips a day, and was associated with a boom-era real estate development on Sanibel. This was actually Sanibel's second ferry, as John Boring, a farmer near Blind Pass, ran a ferry between Sanibel and Captiva before the first Blind Pass Bridge was built. (Courtesy Al and Joy Dobbs)

". . . the [ferry] engines were down under the deck, and of course right where the cars run over top of them, and when there was a car, parked right over the engine . . . I'd have to crawl under the car to get down to tend the engines."

Jerry Lauer
1982 Interview

"NATURE'S MASTERPIECE ON THE GULF"

SANIBEL ISLAND

FORT MYERS

Sanibel Island, opposite the mouth of the beautiful Caloosahatchee river, in the Gulf of Mexico, has a wide sloping beach on the Gulf side and a number of exquisite inlets on the San Carlos Bay side. Sanibel is twelve miles in length and an average of two miles width.

The Cogdell Developments—SUNILAND Beach and LANTANA DEL MAR have a combined beach frontage of over three thousand feet with a depth of one half mile.

Destined to shortly become the tropical west coast playground and the beauty spot of the Gulf section, property values have steadily risen since the Cogdell developments have actually been started. And with Fort Myers fast becoming the metropolis of the South West Coast, SANIBEL offers the truly tropical and romantic of all Florida's water fronts.

With your own car, or our busses, leave wonderful Fort Myers, drive on paved roads to Punta Rassa at the mouth of the Caloosahatchee, transfer the car and yourself to the Cogdell Ferry Boat, over the beautiful bay to SANIBEL ISLAND in a few minutes.

Send NOW for our beautifully illustrated three color literature and full information covering home-sites and investment in this, the wonder section of South West Florida.

ADDRESS

The Cogdell Development Company
W. E. COGDELL, President
FORT MYERS, Florida

The Cogdell Development Company ad, 1926.

Ruth Rutland and niece Barbara Wiles pose on a Sanibel dock circa 1926.

The Blind Pass Bridge in January 1926, photo taken by Cornelius Vanderbilt Jr. When the bridge was built in 1918, the location and plans had to be approved by the War Department in Washington, D.C. The eleven-foot-wide bridge was eight feet above high water. (Courtesy Historical Museum of Southern Florida)

Below: The Mitchell family donated land for the non-denominational community church built in 1917. It was known as the little brown church. As seen here, the 1926 hurricane had damaged the structure, but the storm did more damage to Sanibel farming. Salt water contaminated fields, and the railroad expansion south of Fort Myers meant small island farms would never regain their market advantage. Water transportation was being replaced by rail. (Courtesy Betty Anholt)

Left: Loaded, the *Gladys* steams between stops on her route. From Fort Myers, leaving at 7:00 A.M., stops included Poincetta, Iona, Punta Rassa, Matthews Wharf, Reed's Dock, St. James City, Wulfert, Captiva, and Pineland before noon, reversing her route in the afternoon to return to 5:00 P.M. Passengers, freight, and mail were aboard.

Sam Woodring, son of the homesteader, right, was a well-known fishing guide on Useppa and Sanibel. With the tacit approval of most, he supplied islanders with bootleg spirits during Prohibition. He was also a generous supporter of many community projects, such as building the Community House. Lighthouse keeper Roscoe ("Mac") McLane greets Sam in typical camaraderie. (Courtesy Al and Joy Dobbs)

"Sam never sold you any bad hooch, he brought it over from Cuba and if you bought it from him you knew it was good stuff."

J. Howard Wood
1979 Interview

". . . a fisherman could go fishing, take his catch down there, take them to the fish house, and bring [Sam Woodring] the ticket and he'd give them liquor for it. He had more fishing poles than anybody and never would fish."

John Peurifoy
1979 Interview

Sam Woodring and "Dad" White talking at Woodring Point. (Courtesy Ralph Woodring)

The runboat *Ray*, and several others, carried iced fish to Punta Gorda where boxcar-loads went north. Ice in 300-pound blocks and other supplies were dropped off at the fishhouses as the runboat picked up the waiting fish. The runboat's schedule brought it to a fishhouse every other day.

The passes and bayous were being fished intensively in the 1920s. Not all the fish was meant for the table, much became fertilizer. Boatloads of fish were transshipped to fishhouses where the catch was iced down until the runboat arrived.

United States Light House Service boat, used to maintain channel markers and navigational aids. Assistant Keeper Mac McLane (left) and Jerry Lauer grained the thirty-pound jewfish seen here. During the eye of the 1926 hurricane Jerry Lauer helped the keeper re-anchor the tender, which had "broken loose and drifted into the bushes" [the mangroves] in Tarpon Bay. On getting around in the storm Lauer said, "Once we were walking the right way it was easy!" (Courtesy Al and Joy Dobbs)

Jerry Lauer stands on the deck of the lighthouse boat. The picture was taken from the range light structure which marked the bay channel near Punta Rassa. The range lights were a pair of towers which a boat captain aligned one behind the other so that his vessel was in the channel. They were lit at night and painted white for a day marker. Keeper Bob England noted the practicality of the white paint. He said the birds which constantly roosted on the structure helped maintain its color. (Courtesy Al and Joy Dobbs)

Sanibel Light from the dock, 1926. Porches are partially screened and vegetation is kept minimal to reduce mosquito infestation. A keeper could watch the sun set twice at the lighthouse. First from the ground, then he could see it setting the second time by running up the 127 stairs to the top of the tower. (Courtesy Al and Joy Dobbs)

"From our cottage [Donax and Gulf Drive] we could see the lighthouse because all there was were scrub palmetto and sabal palms."

Elise Fuller
1978 Interview

The crew of the Cuban fishing smack *Santa Lucia* off Point Ybel in 1925. Captain Domingo Hererez's (standing right rear) crew were Pedro, Franco, Fabien, Pete, and Carlos. (Courtesy Ron McCoy)

William Demere, driving, was Lighthouse Keeper in 1926, and seems to have sold property on the side. Jerry Lauer, in back, lived at Assistant Keeper McLane's quarters for a period, helping at the light and eating meals in the Demere quarters. (Courtesy Al and Joy Dobbs)

Mr. and Mrs. Wilson, the school teacher's parents, and the Kinzie steamer *Dixie*, 1926. Mr. Wilson came to Sanibel to improve his health. He suffered from rheumatism, and always attributed his subsequent good health to Sanibel. He was a lawyer who invested in island property and, with his daughter, went through the 1926 hurricane. Mrs. Wilson couldn't stand the heat and bugs, and had returned to Gulfport, Mississippi. While here, Mr. Wilson gardened, and his daughter remarked in 1991 that tomatoes grown on Sanibel before 1926 were the best and sweetest she has ever eaten. (Courtesy Lois Marcott)

Stella Belle Wilson, age eighteen in 1926, in front of her school. Sanibel was her first teaching assignment. She had nine students—three in eighth grade, two in fifth, and one each in sixth, fourth, third, and first grades. (Courtesy Lois Marcott)

The schoolbell and belfry still existed in 1926 before the big storm. When the bell disappeared has become a mystery. Some speculate hurricane destruction, others believe it was melted down in a metal drive during World War II, and some think the bell still exists. The chimney between the second and third windows was added between 1915 and 1926. It is now within the added "second room" of the school. (Courtesy Lois Marcott)

Photographed in 1926, the Wilson farmhouse was on the main road, now Periwinkle. (Courtesy Lois Marcott)

A stylish winter resident, Peggy Sawyer, poses by the Crown gasoline pump on Bailey's dock in 1925. Gas was brought down the Caloosahatchee in fifty-five-gallon drums, deposited into a 300-gallon retaining tank, and pumped to the dock. Vehicles drove onto the dock to refuel. (Courtesy Ron McCoy)

Lillian and David Veenschoten take a break on a fishing trip, 1928. Lillian is seated on what may be the remnants of a homesteader's cat-walk to the water. A cast net hangs from a branch to dry. (Courtesy John and Muriel Veenschoten)

Captain Belton Johnson, son of a homesteading farmer, became a pre-eminent Sanibel fishing guide. He stirs the fire to roast some oysters (foreground) for Vincent Veenschoten (seated rear, hands behind head) and party. The stoneware jug was nearby. Picnics in the mangrove forest, complete with copious liquid refreshment, were popular pastimes and often featured coon oyster roasts and other seafood gathered for the party. Coon oysters grow like great pendulum weights on red mangrove prop roots, which, broken off, provide a convenient handle for suspending the treats in the fire. (Courtesy John and Muriel Veenschoten)

Belton Johnson secures his boat as William, Vincent, John and Lillian Veenschoten await the photographer in 1928. (Courtesy John and Muriel Veenschoten)

FORM 742PQCA

UNITED STATES DEPARTMENT OF AGRICULTURE
PLANT QUARANTINE AND CONTROL ADMINISTRATION
In Co-operation With The State Plant Board of Florida
PROPERTY CERTIFICATE

Farm ~~Grove~~ No. *245-56*

County *Lee*

Place *Sanibel, Fla*

Date *11-20-29*

Owner *C. O. Rutland*

Address *Sanibel, Fla*

Agent _____

Address _____

Location of Property *SW ¼ Sec 24-46-22*

Zone status *3*

Number of Acres *12*

Fruit or Vegetables *Vegetables*

This is to certify that the above described property has been carefully inspected and no evidence has been found of infestation by the Mediterranean fruit fly and the grove is being handled in accordance with the requirments of the State Plant Board.

The *Grower or any certified* Located at *Lee County*
(Name of Packing House or Processing Plant) *Packing House*
is hereby authorized to pick, pack and ship the above fruit or vegetables in accordance with Rules and Regulations of the Plant Quarantine and Control Administration, United States Department of Agriculture, and State Plant Board of Florida.

This certificate is valid until April 1, 1930 for citrus and June 15, 1930 for host vegetables unless revoked for cause.

Approved:
WILMON NEWELL, In Charge,
Mediterranean Fruit Fly Eradication.
Orlando Florida.

H. Jackson
Agent

As is apparent from Clarence Rutland's 1929 quarantine inspection certificate, the Mediterranean fruit fly has long been a Florida farmer's problem. Rutland farmed and held many other jobs, including that of assistant lighthouse keeper. He attributed his penchant for keeping a tidy house to that experience. He purchased his island home in 1928, living there until his death in 1982. In 1984 it was moved to become the Sanibel Historical Museum. The house was built by W. D. Swint in 1913.

Chapter Five

For centuries Sanibel had been the first landfall as ships approached southwest Florida from the Gulf. Now water transportation became marginal, and Sanibel became the hinterland instead of the headland. Auto and rail roads replaced water routes for the traveller, and a trip to the barrier islands had to be specially planned. Other places beckoned once the Tamiami Trail connected the two Florida coasts. In other places the coast was significantly closer to the road

Depression and War

(1929–1945)

now travelled. Sanibel was often unnoticed by the few travellers who ventured south during the Depression and War years.

Visitors came largely because of the birds, shells, and tropical atmosphere. Many visitors and winter residents were scientists, amateur or professional. Dr. Louise Perry studied mollusks, fiddler and horseshoe crabs, fish, and many other creatures. Margaret Storey published often-cited papers on winter freezes, red tide, and fish. Both women travelled to Lake Okeechobee to study fossil shells. Ethel Snyder published on shells and Florida trees. Dr. Frank Craighead examined the island's botany, Dr. George Cooley recorded its plants, Dr. John Goggin chronicled shell mound remains, and many others studied birdlife, geology, entomology, and more. "Ding" Darling came each winter, and his determination to preserve the islands' diversity became a great legacy. Edna St. Vincent Millay and many others came for the abundance of shells. Writers and artists came for the isolation and quiet beauty.

In the middle 1930s a winter-season newspaper reported on island doings. It referred to the island as "The Last Frontier of Rustic Simplicity." Much of the paper was social news, but one constant was complaints to the county on the condition of the island roads. Once it reported praise about the shell road, and continued, "while he is a politician Mr. H. apparently meant what he said." Another constant was science education, and fishing news. A ghost crab "was seen leaping a foot in the air trying to catch a butterfly," and the fact was immortalized.

Marjory Stoneman Douglas submitted poetry. Two titles published were "To a Buzzard Swinging in Silence" and the entirely appropriate "I Am the Mangrove." A reporter wrote [1936] how "Captain A. L. Kinzie . . . can tell tales of the days when the islands were prosperous, raising fruits and vegetables for the early market. . . . now even the buildings that used to house the farmers and their families, are disappearing, falling down or burned by the grass fires that may wreak much damage." There were still reports of tomatoes and peppers being shipped, although the quantities were much diminished.

Commercial shelling was increasing. Complaints were lodged about tons of shells hauled off by truck and trailer. Florida had a state shellfish patrol inspection of the local waters to study shell habits. Sanibel's Shell Fair had become so popular that Fort Myers suggested renaming it "West Coast Shell Fair." Sanibel declined the change.

In 1937 the ferry moved to a new slip closer to the lighthouse, saving travel time across the bay. Work began on a rest room and soft drink parlor, "to serve as a shelter for pedestrians awaiting the ferry." "Mrs. Webb Shanahan . . . well known to all resorters for her operation of the former Palms Hotel, will be in charge of the building." The Palms had been destroyed in a 1936 fire. Unfortunately Pearl Shanahan died before she could make her mark on the new restaurant.

In 1939 Sanibel's population was one hundred, Wulfert still had ten residents. Captiva claimed forty-five. Once World War II began the population slipped even farther. Wulfert was a ghost town, and the north end of the island was turned into a bombing range. Patrols walked the beaches looking for submarines and possible enemy infiltrators. One radio patrolman stationed in a tent on Bowman's Beach described the island as a jungle wilderness. He said, "There are about a dozen civilians on the island ranging in age all the way from seventy to ninety. So our social activity is in the (0) brackets." He spent his spare time swimming and snacking on "native oranges, grapefruit, and cocoanuts. In fact the milk of the cocoanuts, furnishes us with all our drinking water . . ."

In October 1944 the islands experienced a strong hurricane from the south whose winds reportedly peaked at 163 miles per hour. Cuban fishing smacks anchored off the island and the crews came ashore for protection. About forty people found shelter with the lighthouse keeper and his family, Spanish and English speakers both. As the storm raged through the night waves pounded on the quarters floorboards, and the decision was made to go to the lighthouse tower for more security from the storm. The refugees spent the night singing to the accompaniment of a guitar, sitting on the metal spiral stairs of the tower, feeling the sway of the tube from the fierce winds. Up by the Community House the water was knee-deep on the road from high tides and rain. The vegetation was stripped away, but the lighthouse, and the island, had weathered another storm. And the war was soon to be over.

The Sanibel Community House was built in the late 1920s by a number of islanders, on land donated by the Nutt family. The Association's Charter was written in 1928. Its By-Laws state its purpose: "The Sanibel Community Association is composed of neighbors joined to do what none could do alone. The Association works for the civic, social, educational and recreational well being of the entire community. Evermindful that this is an island community, fragile in nature, unique in history and character, we are obligated to ourselves and to our posterity to maintain a community proud of its heritage, responsive to its problems and confident of its future." This photo taken in 1929 shows work still in progress. Notice the privy at rear. (Courtesy Gertrude Bergin)

John Veenschoten is ready for high water with a bucket and boots, about 1929. His brother David and father Vincent watch from the porch. (Courtesy John and Muriel Veenschoten)

The Sawyer Cottage with Fanny, John (inside car), Vincent and Lillian Veenschoten, and a guest, stopped in front. In the mid-1940s the house became Ethel Snyder's home and gift shop. Snyder also became a writer and regional naturalist. (Courtesy John and Muriel Veenschoten)

The "Beach House" in its original location near the Island Inn about 1938. (Courtesy John and Muriel Veenschoten)

The Hennings family stops at the Florida border inspection station in 1929. This homemade trailer was used by the family into the 1980s. Agricultural inspections of vehicles continue today. Auto trips to Florida could be arduous, but roadside picnic lunches were pleasant respites along the isolated narrow roads. (Courtesy Gertrude Bergin)

The *Best* docks by the Bailey Store on Sanibel about 1929. The Hennings' car and trailer are aboard, bringing from Kentucky the household goods needed for their winter stay on the island. (Courtesy Gertrude Bergin)

Mrs. Stewart sits at the wheel of the "school bus" about 1930 in front of Sanibel School. The Stewarts, a family of eight, farmed near the present Gulf Pines subdivision. The Hennings children beside the "bus"—a 1927 or 1928 Chevrolet—are (left to right): George Jr., Gertrude, and Robert. (Courtesy Gertrude Bergin)

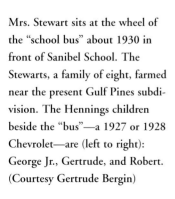

The Ross Mayer family pose in their touring car in front of Shorehaven about 1930. Left to right are: J. Ross Mayer, Sr., Betty, Grace, and J. Ross Jr. in mother Daisy Mayer's lap. The family built Shorehaven, a Sears Roebuck catalog house, on San Carlos Bay about 1925. The house was prefabricated with each piece marked for assembly. Weather was rough the day delivery was made, and some pieces had to be rescued from the bay, but all went together well. Although altered, the house remains on its original location today, as does another Sears prefabricated house nearby, Morning Glories. (Courtesy Elinore Dormer)

Right: Captain Leon Crumpler with his trademark bow tie (right) and Henry the engineer on the ferry *Best*, April 1932. (Courtesy Elinore Dormer)

"I got after Kinzie . . . to buy it [the Cogdell ferry]. Well, they weren't interested in the ferries because they'd had a diesel engine in it, old time diesel engine, and they were steamboat people."

Leon Crumpler
1968 Interview

Sanibel ferry.

Miss Charlotta's Tea Room on San Carlos Bay in the early 1930s. Built to be a gas station, the building temporarily became the store after the wharf and original store were destroyed in the 1926 storm. Bailey's General Store was then rebuilt on adjoining land. Left to right: Miss Kate Matthews, Mrs. Albert Willis with Sam Bailey, Grannie Matthews, and Annie Meade Bailey. The building is now a part of the Sanibel Historical Village and Museum.

Left: John (J. W.) Mitchell and his mule Jenny meet an automobile on a grassy Sanibel road.

Below: On the Blind Pass bridge, Dean Mitchell displays his four dozen sheepshead.

Edmund and Elnora Gavin, 1933. Their marriage united the Gavin family which settled on Sanibel in the early 1920s with the Walker family following a short time later.

Sam, Francis, and John Bailey on their father's farm mule. John Bailey said their father came to the island with nothing, arriving in 1894 by steamboat at the post office landing, and it was eighteen months before he left the island the first time. His father told him "if there was anyway on God's green earth that he could [have] turn[ed] around and gone anywhere else he would've." Frank Bailey eventually farmed as much as six hundred acres.

Before the advent of monofilament line, net fishermen spent much of their non-fishing time drying, inspecting, repairing, and treating their nets, which were usually made of cotton or flax. They might be tarred or limed for preservation. These net houses and spreads were on Woodring Point, shown in 1934. (Courtesy Ralph Woodring)

The intersection of Tarpon Bay Road and "Periwinkle" in 1936, with the Cooper Place in the distance (then owned by John Bruaw).

The Burnap Cottage was built before the turn of the century of Woodring Point, and purchased by Hiram Burnap, a Toledo businessman. Mainly used as a winter residence, in 1935 when this photo was taken, it was owned by Mabel Critchley. When the Brewsters purchased it in 1948, they expanded the back and added a second floor. In 1995 the cottage was moved to the Sanibel Historical Village and Museum, and has been restored to its original layout.

Right: Forward of the wheelhouse, Annie Meade Bailey looks ahead while son John watches the wheelman. Grannie Matthews is directly behind John, and Francis Bailey is perched next to Captain George Kinzie. Sam Bailey is at the side of the wheelhouse. The others are unknown.

Ferry schedule, 1936. Until January 1937 the ferry landed at the dock at Bailey's General Store. The move farther east saved time and made navigation easier for the ferries, and allowed the Kinzie Brothers to operate a restaurant on their property. In 1936 the Singleton Brothers began their mailboat operation and the era of the wood-burning steamers ended when the *Gladys* sank.

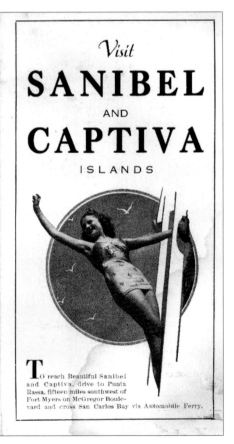

1936

FERRY SCHEDULE
★

Leave Punta Rassa:
    8:00 - 9:30 - 11:00 A. M.
    1:30 - 3:00 - 4:30 P. M.

Leave Sanibel Island:
    8:45 - 10:15 - 11:45 A. M.
    2:15 - 3:45 - 5:15 P. M.

During busy tourist season, trips will be increased to accommodate the demand by running oftener and later. From May 1st to December 31st, the trips leaving Punta Rassa at 9:30 a. m. and 1:30 and 3:00 p. m., may be omitted depending on the requirements of traffic.

★

INFORMATION BUREAU
1118 FIRST STREET

KINZIE BROTHERS STEAMER LINE
Telephone 489 or 185
FORT MYERS . . FLORIDA

Visit
SANIBEL
AND
CAPTIVA
ISLANDS

To reach Beautiful Sanibel and Captiva, drive to Punta Rassa, fifteen miles southwest of Fort Myers on McGregor Boulevard and cross San Carlos Bay via Automobile Ferry.

Ferry approaching the Kinzie Dock near the lighthouse. The stage of the tide and direction of current could make loading and unloading difficult.

Webb Shanahan plays with a pet monkey. Perhaps he is taking a break from gathering seagrapes, which makes an excellent island jelly.

Webb Shanahan with daughter Katharine, known as "Snookie." Webb was two years old when he came to Sanibel with his family from Key West so that his father Henry Shanahan could become Assistant Lighthouse Keeper. Henry Shanahan's wife died in 1895. That year Othman and Irene Rutland and their children moved to Sanibel because the Great Florida Freeze had destroyed his groves in Apopka. Othman died in 1899, and the Shanahan and Rutland families merged when Henry married Irene. They added one more child to the dozen in the combined family. Webb eventually married his stepsister Pearlie.

Mrs. Webb (Pearl) Shanahan. (Courtesy Al and Joy Dobbs)

95

RATES: $4.50 PER DAY. $28 PER WEEK. $26 PER WEEK, BY MONTH
CHILDREN FULL PRICE

Palm Lodge
SANIBEL, FLORIDA

A. C. L. R'Y. JACKSONVILLE TO FORT MYERS
DAILY STEAMER SERVICE FORT MYERS TO SANIBEL

GOOD BATHING
FINE SHELLING
SPLENDID FISHING
EXCELLENT CUISINE

FOR PARTICULARS WRITE
MRS. H. SHANAHAN,
SANIBEL, FLORIDA

This circa 1926 Palm Lodge business card mentions steamer service. The wood-burning steamers *Gladys* and *Dixie* delivered mail and passengers from Fort Myers before the ferry began operation. (Courtesy Al and Joy Dobbs)

Palm Lodge, later known as The Palms. Pearl Rutland Shanahan and her mother Irene Rutland (Mrs. Henry) Shanahan ran the hotel. Pearl's husband Webb was Sanibel's mail carrier, first by pony and later by car. Although plans were drawn to rebuild The Palms after the fire, construction never got underway.

Edna St. Vincent Millay, 1937. (Courtesy Special Collection, Vassar College Libraries, Poughkeepsie, New York)

When the poet and her husband Eugen Boissevain visited Sanibel to add to her collection of shells May 2, 1936, they had not expected the trip to have long-lasting consequences. They arrived on the last ferry, checked in at The Palms, and had the luggage sent up to the room while they went out on the beach for shelling. When they looked back toward the hotel a short time later they saw it in flames. The building and contents were completely destroyed, reportedly by a faulty oil burner. Some guests barely escaped, tying sheets together to get out of a second-story window. The Boissevains lost everything they had with them except the clothes on their backs and their auto. She referred to a cherished seventeenth-century copy of *Catullus* as her only "emotional" loss, though a "handsome" emerald ring and the entire and only manuscript of *Conversation at Midnight*, which she had just completed, were also consumed by the fire. Millay later wrote that "swathed in something which once had been a white linen suit, and wrapped in a rug in lieu of a coat . . . [w]e were so painfully unpresentable that we slunk into hotels late at night with our arms over our faces, and sneaked out before daybreak" on their return trip to Steepletop, their New York farm. She spent the next year reconstructing the burned manuscript.

Only a small kitchenless cottage remained on the grounds of "The Palms," as the hotel was known before it burned. Webb Shanahan stands in its yard with two women, probably wife Pearl and mother Irene. (Courtesy Al and Joy Dobbs)

Carl Jordan, age six, and his uncle Nathaniel Walker in 1938. Born on Sanibel in 1932, lifelong resident Jordan recalled his summer job of gathering shells, usually for $1 per bushel. Pectens, though, fetched $8 per bushel.

Lighthouse Keeper Roscoe "Mac" McLane, 1934. McLane died at age thirty-eight in 1938 after an emergency operation for appendicitis.

William Demeritt was Superintendent of the Seventh Lighthouse District, headquartered in Key West. The district encompassed stations from St. Marks on Florida's Panhandle to Jupiter on the east coast.

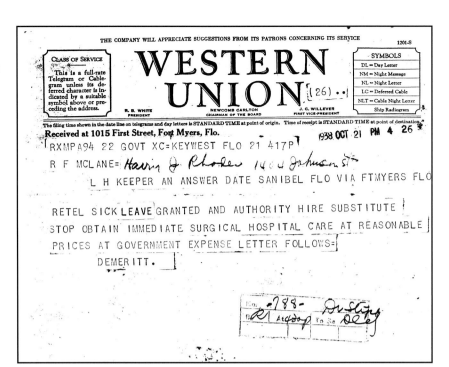

Tarpon hunters at Blind Pass.

Blind Pass swarmed with mullet in 1939.

Right: Captiva winter residents Jay Darling, Alice O'Brien, and Penny Darling about 1940. All were instrumental in the creation of the Sanibel National Wildlife Refuge in 1945. Miss O'Brien was a mechanic during World War I, a navigator, fisherman, animal lover, and leading St. Paul citizen. Mr. Darling's interests in conservation issues were lifelong, deeply felt, and widely published. During the record-breaking 1947 red tide outbreak, Darling lobbied hard for government investigation of the phenomenon.

Frank Bailey in the late 1930s. One of three brothers—Ernest, Harry, and Frank—he and Annie Meade Matthews Bailey had three sons, Francis, Jr. John, and Sam. Mrs. Bailey died in 1935. Frank Bailey operated the family store and raised his boys. He served as Justice of the Peace on Sanibel, an elected position. He died in 1952. He said he wanted his tombstone epitaph to read, "He was fair," and it was a judgment islanders believed he had earned in full measure.

License for the Casa Marina restaurant at the new ferry landing near the lighthouse, 1939.

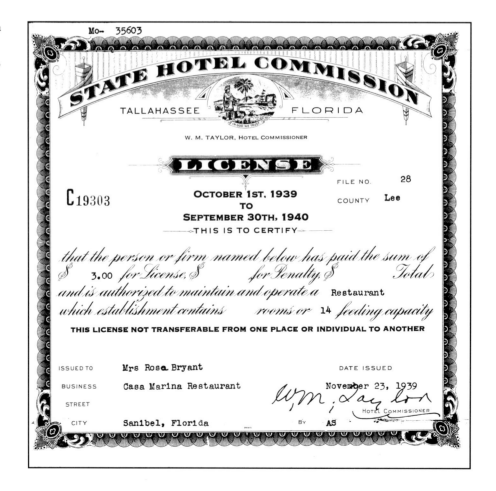

The *Islander* loads while the *Best* waits. Kinzie's second ferry, the *Islander* could hold up to twenty cars but didn't stay long on San Carlos Bay. Two years after it began its run in 1939, it was requisitioned by the government as a troop transport during World War II. The *Best* continued alone as before shuttling islanders across the bay.

John Bruaw and his Model T truck, 1939.

By the late 1930s—the right front fender of a 1937 Chevrolet is visible—Sanibel School had expanded to two rooms and more windows had been added so sufficient sunlight came over the students' shoulders. While the belfry is gone the roofline remains steep. The flagpole stands by the steps. (Courtesy Gertrude Bergin)

"Miss McCann [schoolhouse teacher would] pitch, and she had a system if you were a little kid you got five strikes, if you were a little bigger you got four strikes, and if you were big enough to play regular baseball you got three strikes. That kinda evened it up."

Willis Combs
1977 Interview

Daisy Mayer loved to fish from the dock of her home, Shorehaven. (Courtesy Elinore Dormer)

[Daisy Mayer] . . . had one of the few houses on the Bay and she always left a light on her porch at night so the people on the boats could find their way in."

Jo Pickens
1992 Interview

Transferring iced mullet and sheepshead onto a runboat. (Copyright Charles McCullough)

Tarpon Bay fishhouse. (Copyright Charles McCullough)

Esperanza and Sam Woodring share a moment with their puppy. Jerry Lauer described a typical visit to Sam's to purchase a bottle. He would go to the end of the road and turn his car facing out so he didn't have to make that maneuver in an "impaired" condition. A walk across the boardwalk led to the yard, where he and Sam would sit, converse, and share a companionable glass. At some point in the conversation Sam might say, "See that box over there? What you've ordered is under there." Eventually Jerry would go on about his business without Sam's ever handling the merchandise. (Courtesy Ralph Woodring)

"When the mullet were running. . . . Now, you are not going to believe this, but . . . he would catch whatever he wanted to eat the next day with a pitchfork. . . . You see, they were running from these other big fish that were on the outside. . . . They were right up [close to the beach] most especially on moonlight nights."

Esperanza Woodring
1990 Interview

103

A fishing party with Esperanza Wood-ring (center) in Tarpon Bay. Edwin Colby is far right. In the right background is Harrison Woodring's stilt house near Green Point. John Morris, son of Flora and John Morris, loved visiting there, feasting on a breakfast of freshly caught mullet roe and grits with his uncle.

[Esperanza Woodring] "knows more about fishing than the majority of these men around here that claim they have known it all their lives. But she's known it all her life too, don't kid yourself she hasn't."

Clarence Rutland
1979 Interview

A U.S. Army patrol boat docks at Captiva during World War II. Army personnel patrolled Sanibel and Captiva beaches during the war, and blackout conditions were enforced on the islands. (Courtesy Gertrude Bergin)

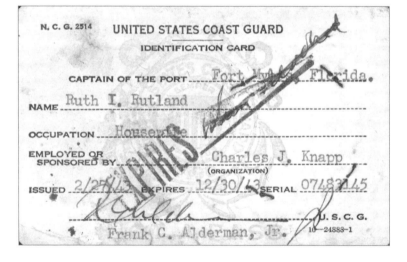

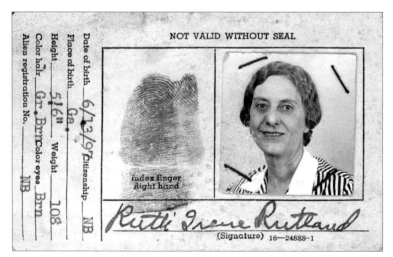

This Point Ybel aerial shows the dormitory quarters and observation tower as well as both lighthouse quarters, the light tower, and the lighthouse dock and boathouse. The road from upper right bends toward the Gulf to reach the lighthouse, passing the site of the Palms Hotel by the clump of Australian pines. The straight line of pines marks the Kinzie Brothers ferry landing property from bayside to their Gulfside Park. The vegetation on the point is largely mangrove, and beyond the ferry landing, prairie grass becomes prominent. (Courtesy United States Coast Guard)

Left: During the second World War, the United States Coast Guard issued identification cards to island residents due to fears of enemy infiltration via submarines and rafts. Sanibel's isolation was emphasized by its low population, fewer than one hundred. Farming and tourism had practically ceased and many were serving in the armed forces.

Wash day at the Light Station. The twin water towers are
visible between the pump house and light tower in this
February 1943 photo. (Courtesy United States Coast
Guard)

Lighthouse quarters No. 2, occupied by the Assistant Lighthouse Keeper. The construction materials in the foreground may have been for repairs on the septic tank drainfield, which was installed at this spot in 1925. The submarine observation tower is to the right of the building. The rainwater cistern beside the porch of the quarters was destroyed in the 1944 storm. Gulf-side porch stairs still exist in the photo. (Courtesy United States Coast Guard)

(GI-7781-BPS)(2-6-43-4P)(6 3/8)BAAFFUS... MYERS FLA.
BLDG. GASPARILLA ISLAND FLA.

Personnel stroll across the yard at the Light during World War II. Notice the twin stairway which leads from each quarters to the base of the lighthouse tower. It was via this stair that a group of hurricane refugees trapped in the quarters by the 1944 storm managed to make their way to the tower. Storm waves crashed against the quarter's floorboards, leading the group to believe the buildings might wash away. About forty people including a number of Cuban fishermen survived the night seated on the spiral staircase in the lighthouse tube, singing songs and playing a guitar to comfort themselves and the children. The stairs were removed in 1951. (Courtesy United States Coast Guard)

Sanibel Light, from the Gulf. The bird-dominated pilings were placed for a construction dock during World War II, when the submarine observation tower (right) and dormitory quarters were built behind the easternmost lighthouse quarters. The pilings disappeared during the 1944 hurricane.

The remains of the pumphouse after the 1944 storm. The quarters stairs are visible at middle left. In a 1947 storm Bosun Mate Bob England and his wife Mae shared their quarters with some Cuban fishermen needing refuge. The stairs were torn off by that storm as well, and washed away. Mrs. England was within two weeks of giving birth, and the Cubans would not leave to repair their ship until they replaced the steps. They did not want the Señora trapped in the building in her condition with no way to ground. (Courtesy United States Coast Guard)

[In the 1944 hurricane we stayed in the lighthouse tower overnight.] "There was definite movement to it. You could feel it sway and swing in the wind as it came along."

Pearl Stokes
1982 Interview

Right: Sara Lauer and neighbors Hazel (Reed) and Joe Godard pluck a bird in the back yard. Hazel Godard became postmaster from 1940 to 1943 after her father retired from the position. (Courtesy Al and Joy Dobbs)

Sanibel pioneer Lettie Nutt survived her sisters, dying at age eighty-six in 1945. (Courtesy Florence Young)

Sanibel farmer and homesteader (1888) Nels Holt. He married Nannie Nutt in 1913, "late in life." He had long been infatuated with her but feared to express himself. Nannie was the only one of Letitia Nutt's three daughters to marry. Born in Malmo, Sweden, Nels Holt was eighty-six when he died in 1947 and is buried in the Nutt family plot at Gray Gables. (Courtesy Florence Young)

Right: "Snookie" Shanahan cuts her Uncle Clarence's hair, one of many jobs islanders took for granted. Islanders relied on each other in childbirth and for everything from tooth-pulling to fire-fighting to child-raising.

Taken prior to 1951, when the ramp to the boathouse was removed, this view of the lighthouse complex indicates the point extended well east of its current position. The last official keeper of the light was Chief Bosun Mate William Robert England. His title was "United States Coast Guard Officer-in-charge of Sanibel Island Light Attendant Station." He and his assistants were responsible for twenty-three lights and 153 day beacons in Pine Island Sound, up the Caloosahatchee to the present location of the locks, and to Fort Myers Beach. (Courtesy United States Coast Guard)

Chapter Six

After World War II the nation's economy expanded. Soldiers who travelled during the war were eager to show Florida to their families left at home. Sanibel had remained forgotten for nearly twenty years, but now the island was rediscovered. People came to fish, shell, and walk the beach. They needed accommodations for their families and a place to park their cars. Mom-and-Pop motels began to appear, shops opened, real estate began to sell, restaurants opened.

Growing Again

(1946–1959)

The Kinzies added ferries. In June, 1950, the Intercounty Telephone Company connected a telephone line to "the other side" at the ferry landing. In September of 1950, again at the ferry landing, Sanibel mosquitoes set a new world record when a lone New Jersey light trap collected 365,000 mosquitoes in a single night.

In 1947 a significant hurricane damaged the lighthouse quarters, and the Coast Guard decided that it was an unacceptable risk to continue to man the light when it could be automated. They concluded they could tend the light and channel markers from Fort Myers without personnel being subjected to the danger of storms. When the last resident lighthouse keeper was restationed in Fort Myers in 1949, the Sanibel National Wildlife Refuge took over the lighthouse quarters for an office and residence for refuge manager Tom Wood.

Nineteen forty-seven was a year of floods. That winter a record-setting red tide occurred in southwest Florida. The water was white with dead fish. Dolphins, manatees, and sea turtles washed up along with every type of ray and fish. The virulent water killed every fish one Cuban fishing smack had caught in weeks of work. The captain came ashore to ask Lighthouse Keeper England to verify its catch so its owners would accept the loss. They did not want to be accused of selling the catch themselves or shirking on the job. Once he recorded their catch, tons of dead fish were buried at Point Ybel near the light. Bob England planted a garden over the site, and said the vegetables which resulted, including broccoli, were the best he'd ever seen.

Building and construction continued. Some islanders, like the Hiers, formed their own concrete blocks from beach sand and erected motels or homes. Jack Cole built an open-air restaurant which he expanded as it prospered. No paved roads existed. Pontoon seaplanes taxied up to shore. Casa Ybel opened its grass airfield in 1953. In 1955 the Mosquito Control District started to dig drainage ditches, working east to west. The possibility was discussed of connecting all the islands down the west coast by roads and bridges, similar to the east coast's AIA. One plan even envisioned a "circle tour . . . second to none for waterfront beauty" which would cross from Punta Rassa to Sanibel to Pine Island to Cayo Costa, connecting to Gasparilla and Sanibel-Captiva. These plans would circulate from time to time and then be shelved. The idea did not seem economically feasible.

While island business opportunities expanded, so did concerns about responsible growth. Islanders knew the lessons of Florida's east coast, and did not want to destroy the very ambiance which lured them here. The Sanibel Community Association, and later the Sanibel Island Improvement Association, were concerned about roads, dredging, public dumping, teen activities and other issues. Alligators were found with bullet holes, and conservationists worked to preserve state and county island land for wildlife under a national refuge umbrella.

The Kinzies built a tiny post office near the ferry landing when Scotia Bryant became postmaster in 1944. A decade later a larger building was erected. The salt-water canals on the island's east end were dredged starting in the late 1950s. The main road, now named Periwinkle Way, finally received a layer of asphalt. Wildfires burned in the island interior from time to time, often starting from a tossed cigarette or discarded bottle which acted as a prism. In 1959 the *Algiers*, a converted Mississippi River car ferry turned into a spectacular home for former Congressman Lathrop Brown and his wife, Helen, was brought ashore on land purchased from Louise Perry.

Blind Pass was emptying into the Gulf near Bowman's Beach, nearly two miles from its bridge. The migrating pass captured Clam Bayou and altered the island's north end.

Another alteration for the island was its relationship with Cuba. From the earliest exploration and contact until 1959, Cubans had come to Sanibel to fish, live, and trade. Some fishermen who had lost their lives in storms were buried on Sanibel. Others corresponded with islanders for years. But when Fidel Castro came into power the fishing smacks stopped coming north. The occasional "balsero" or rafter has washed ashore since then, but Sanibel's connection with the island nation to the south was snapped. Sanibel was no longer on the northern fringe of the Caribbean. Now it became a southern beach for the U.S. mainland. Some developers believed the island needed a bridge to that world.

Bob England on the beach surrounded by cold-shocked fish. When the rare freeze hits the islands, fish in our shallow water are vulnerable. The cold wind stirring previously warm seas creates sudden water temperature drops. Whether stunned or killed outright by plummeting temperature, these fish wash ashore with other affected sealife, and remain edible. (Courtesy Bob and Mae England)

Bob England served as Sanibel's last resident Light-house keeper from 1946 to 1949. The large redfish in his wheelbarrow, too big to carry, was a beach find at Point Ybel. England related how big snook and reds would patrol the deep-water swash channel curving around the point. When mullet or other food fish swam by, the predators would rush an attack, sometimes flopping onto the beach from the force of their ambush. England frequently came across marks in the sand where these fish had wiggled back into the water, but this was one that didn't get away. (Courtesy Bob and Mae England)

"December 13, 1934 . . . we had an old wood water tank here, and it froze on the island that night and there were icicles three feet long—or more—hanging off."

Francis Bailey
1973 Interview

Like many other islanders, the Lauer family gathered and cleaned shells from island beaches to sell to wholesalers farther north. These tables set up in the yard were part of the cleaning and sorting operation. The people are identified as Anita, Sandra, and Richard. (Courtesy Al and Joy Dobbs)

A 1948 family gathering on Clarence Rutland's front porch. Clarence Rutland sits at left rear with his brother-in-law Lewis Wiles, and two of Wiles' grandchildren. Front row: Ethel Padgett Longmire (Rutland's niece), Katie Rutland Padgett (sister), "Jose" the dog, Michael Longmire (grandnephew). (Courtesy Ethel Longmire)

Esperanza Woodring cooking fish at Duffy's. Duffy's Creek is one of the several tidal creeks in the J. N. "Ding" Darling National Wildlife Refuge. She holds some mangrove oysters, ready for roasting. (Courtesy Ralph Woodring)

BAY WATER
FISHING GUIDE

Shelling   -   Sightseeing
Wildlife Trips By Boat

More than 30 Years on the Islands

ESPERANZA WOODRING

By Appointment   -   Phone GReenleaf 2-2292

Esperanza Woodring's business card. Born on Cayo Costa in 1901, Esperanza moved to Woodring Point in her teens when she married Sam Woodring, son of homesteader Sam Woodring, Sr. Her family fished commercially, and she met her husband when he was guiding fishermen off Useppa Island. Priscilla Murphy said of her friend Esperanza, "All our fishing guides are gentlemen except one, and she's a lady."

"I wish the islands were given back to the Indians myself. Even now [1977] the rattlesnakes have left."

Esperanza Woodring
1977 Interview

Esperanza Woodring and Tom Wood, Woodring Point neighbors, share a meal of roasted
oysters. Tom Wood became the first refuge manager in 1949, serving until his 1971
retirement, and the Woods lived in a house built by the Woodring family on the Point's
tip. (Courtesy Ralph Woodring)

Olive Rhodes stands beside her school bus in 1951. Mrs. King, wife of Casa Ybel's manager, and daughter Polly are on the right. Mrs. Rhodes would stop the bus when someone spotted a gopher tortoise sunning or crossing the sandy road. She would retrieve the reptile and bring it aboard to take home for her family's cooking pot. (Courtesy Polly Kimball)

Pete King practices on the horse conch trumpet to the amusement of Casa Ybel employee
Ernest (last name unknown), and Pete's sister Polly. Many of the hotel staff in the 1950s
were Bahamian, and the practice of calling guests to dinner via conch shell horn may
have originated with them. However native Calusa also are thought to have blown
conchs. (Courtesy Polly Kimball)

A chickee full of food competes with beach sights and sounds at Casa Ybel Beach. Buffets were held every Friday at noon during the season. Charlie Hurst stands behind the table at far left, while Carl Jordan, right foreground, cooks.

Chester, Casa Ybel chef, and his assistant Berry in his kitchen in 1951. (Courtesy Polly Kimball)

Buddy Bobst, pilot, taxis his plane onto Casa Ybel's beach.
(Courtesy Polly Kimball)

Gulf Airways, Inc. with pilot Buddy Bobst (second from right), was a quick air-taxi away during the 1950s. It was popular entertainment to watch landings and take-offs in the waters surrounding the islands. (Courtesy Polly Kimball)

125

Francis Bailey inside the Bailey General
Store in the early 1950s. In 1991 the
store was moved to become a part of the
Historical Museum complex.

"Dad" White caulks the seams of a boat. (Copyright Charles McCullough)

Eldon ("Dad") White (left) and John ("Pegleg") Dugan on Woodring Point. White was a handyman, working on boats, nets, etc. During the 1944 storm Dugan's wooden leg was found washed ashore, and he was believed lost. The following day he made his way back out of the mangroves where he had been stranded. (Copyright Charles McCullough)

Esperanza Woodring listens to one of the "screw-worm men" while others concentrate on her food in the mid-1950s. "Dad" White stands, Ralph Woodring is second from right. Next to Esperanza is E. F. Knipling, who field-tested his concept of pest control of the screw-worm fly on Sanibel in 1953. Screw-worms were a major cattle industry problem, an infestation able to kill a cow within ten days. Knipling sterilized the flies with x-rays, eventually converting a Sebring, Florida aircraft hangar into a giant "fly factory." His idea, which he worked on despite little encouragement, is now considered by some entomologists to be the most important advance in insect pest control in the twentieth century—perhaps ironic since Knipling was previously head of the USDA research lab that developed DDT during World War II. By irradiation sterilization Knipling eradicated the screw-worm in cattle, and the concept of inundating an infected region with sterile flies has been used with medflies and other agricultural pests since then. (Courtesy Ralph Woodring)

The Sea Horse Shop opened its louvered doors to welcome customers and tropical breezes in January 1954 near the ferry landing. Sanibel's second-oldest retail business, it was the first shop to remain open year-round. Chris (left) and Mary Jo, daughter of owners Joe and Mary Gault (now Bell), stand in front of the shop. (Courtesy Mary Bell)

To raise funds for the fledgling Episcopal church in the mid-1950s, Elise Fuller, Jeane Jack, and Fanetta Stahlin modeled clothes from the Sea Horse Shop at a Casa Ybel fashion show. For some years the Episcopal congregation worshiped in the Casa Marina tearoom before St. Michael's Church was built in 1961. (Courtesy Mary Bell)

A Community House square dance was a popular 1950s get-together. This Christmas dance included Priscilla and Pat Murphy, Jim and Jo Pickens, Dick Kearns, and Clarence Rutland among others. (Courtesy Jim and Jo Pickens)

"We used to sleep, 'cause we had no air conditioning, so you'd sleep with your bed by a window. If you were on the lee side of the building and you'd wake up in the morning and the screen would literally be black with mosquitoes."

Francis Bailey
1992 Interview

Asbestos siding is applied to the lighthouse buildings in 1955. Manager Wood noted the siding was not much more costly than painting and maintenance costs would be much reduced. Notice the screened porch at this time. (Courtesy J. N. "Ding" Darling National Wildlife Refuge)

"I complained about mosquitoes to Uncle Arthur Gibson . . . and he said, 'Well, you'll probably get used to 'um. But, I doubt you'll ever learn to like 'um."

Jim Pickens
1992 Interview

Mosquito control ditches were first dug in 1955, starting at the lighthouse end of the island and working to the west. The ditching was never completed, leading Mosquito Control Director T. Wayne Miller to comment, "We start larvaciding where the ditches stop." (Courtesy J. N. "Ding" Darling National Wildlife Refuge)

In the 1950s the road to the lighthouse and buildings were threatened by erosion. The submarine observation tower had been well away from the shore when built during the second World War, but by the late 1950s it was in danger of being undermined and had tilted significantly. It was dismantled and burned in 1959. The tower's concrete bases remain buried at the point although occasionally they become uncovered.

". . . when I first moved there [1958] in that [lighthouse quarters] house, . . . I could take a cast net and throw it off the porch and fill my net with mullet."

Charles LeBuff
1992 Interview

Waiting in line for the ferry, 1951. Backups occurred in season, as the ferries carried a limited number of cars, though lines didn't build up as long as today's seasonal traffic jams. In the 1950s people left their car in line and conversed or had a sandwich at Casa Marina, the tea room conveniently next to the landing. In summer mosquitoes could be so bad drivers huddled in their cars with windows closed despite the heat. Cars coming off the ferry would accelerate to twenty to twenty-five miles per hour before cranking down their windows to "outrun" the mosquitoes. (Courtesy Polly Kimball)

[In 1950] "I came to stay two weeks, and I stayed eleven. And the Hiers [By-the-Sea-Motel] charged me $91.00 for the whole summer."

Edie Mugridge
1992 Interview

Sanibel ferry landing, 1958. In his 1955 refuge report, Tom Wood, refuge
manager, notes that the ferry brought 33,945 visitors to the refuge from
January through April, and estimated another 1,800 came by boat and plane.

Captain Leon Crumpler was the first and senior ferry captain for the Kinzies. Once Crumpler had talked them into buying the *Best*, the Kinzies decided Crumpler would have to run it. He and his wife Jeannie Clyde lived at Punta Rassa overlooking the ferry route, and later the causeway which replaced it. Clyde Crumpler was the daughter of Sanibel farmers, the Riddles. She also ran a grocery at Punta Rassa. Their home, originally built as part of the Western Union Telegraph complex, was torn down in the early 1990s.

SANIBEL ISLAND FERRY

Winter Schedule

January 1st until April 15th

Leave Punta Rassa:
On the hour and half hour from 7:30 A.M. until 5:00 P.M.

Leave Sanibel:
On the hour and half hour from 8:00 A.M. until 5:30 P.M.

Summer Schedule

April 15th until January 1st

Leave Punta Rassa:
On the hour and half hour from 8:00 A.M. until 5:00 P.M.

Leave Sanibel:
On the hour and half hour from 8:30 A.M. until 5:30 P.M.

This schedule subject to change without notice.

Ferry Rates

Cars and Pick-up Trucks	$1.00 each way
Passengers, Adults	.47 each way
Children, between ages of 6 and 12	.25 each way
Children, under six years	No charge
Trucks over 1-2 ton, with 1-2 ton load	$1.25 each way
Loads over 1-2 ton load	5c per hundred pounds

Government tax included

Special Trips

Special Trips: made in emergencies only and must be arranged for in advance with Captains of Ferries. Rates governed by hour of trip.

Any scheduled trip may be omitted to carry gas trucks. Passengers and cars cannot be hauled with gas trucks. (Federal Law)

Capt. R. T. Chappelle in charge at Punta Rassa

SANIBEL ISLAND FERRY

P. O. Box 189   (Issued August 1958)   Fort My.

Ferry schedule card from 1958.

The process of creating the subdivision of West Rocks began with a dragline digging a canal. Lakes and canals had a two-fold reason for being—not only does the waterway increase the value of property, but the sand from the digging operation raises the elevation of the lot. Much of Sanibel's geology was "improved" by such terraforming in the 1950s. On a much larger scale, developers were following the lead of the Calusa who were expert centuries earlier in building mounds and cutting canals.

Wildfires have been a significant part of Sanibel's ecology, whether they resulted from lightning strike or were human-caused. In winter's dry season a spark sometimes precipitated fires which burned out of control for days in the central slough wetlands. Firefighters were island volunteers, although by the mid-1950s Sanibel had acquired a firetruck. This blaze in the vicinity of the Rocks subdivision was not unusual. (Courtesy John and Muriel Veenschoten)

"The biggest risk we had in the early days was fires . . . the whole interior of the island . . . in those days was just sawgrass. Sometimes it wouldn't rain all winter, and if somebody dropped a cigarette butt in that, the fire would go for two or three miles."

J. Howard Wood
1979 Interview

When Bob and Cookie Dugger began to build their Tropical Village on West Gulf Drive, they needed fill dirt for some of the slough areas. As was standard practice for 1957, they took the dragline and dump truck to the Gulf beach and hauled sand to their site. This informal practice was halted in 1962 when Jamestown Metal Products (Beachview) was cited by the state and by the Army Corps of Engineers for beach dredging. The scale of such sand removal had become too large to ignore. Additionally, Hugo Lindgren, owner of Jamestown, had become the focus of a firestorm of controversy concerning the causeway construction.

The bird tower in the Bailey Tract was built in 1954 by builders James S. Pickens and J. Broward Keene (a former assistant at the lighthouse).

A traditional outdoor buffet at Island Inn.

This late 1950s aerial view of
the new (1954) concrete Blind
Pass bridge also shows the Casta-
ways Marina and Resort in the
foreground. The Turner's Beach
"tail" of Captiva extends off the
photo to the left, all eroded
by the mid-1970s. Roosevelt
Channel, named after President
Theodore Roosevelt, snakes
down to the Pass from the upper
right, curving around the lower
part of Buck Key. (Courtesy Jean
Culpepper)

Postmistress Scotia Bryant at the Sanibel Post Office at the ferry landing, early 1950s.
Scotia served as postmistress from 1943 to 1967. Ethel Snyder said three was a crowd in
this structure. It was replaced by a larger building in 1954. In 1965 Snyder said, "The little old post office got trundled away on the back of a truck right down the main road and
into oblivion. . . . What the public doesn't know is that it is doing very nicely, thank you,
as a home for chickens. No fluttering of flags, just fluttering of feathers. . . ." When
Scotia began handling mail, she sorted for seventy-five year-round residents. Population
climbed rapidly through her tenure. After Bryant's retirement the post office returned to
Tarpon Bay Road, adjacent to the old Cooper homestead where in the 1880s mail was
first distributed by Captain George Cooper. (Courtesy John Veenschoten)

The road from the ferry landing to Casa Ybel and Captiva, 1952. Road paving was still several years in the future. (Courtesy John Veenschoten)

"The story was that if you went from Sanibel to Captiva, you could pick up enough car parts to build you a car at the other end."

Mary Aleck
1992 Interview

"A friend of mine . . . once said to me, 'You know, I've never been in a place that I liked where they had good roads.' There's a lot of truth in that."

George Tenney

[Captiva people from the last ferry would] "come by our house just a speeding, to see who was going to get on that [unpaved San-Cap] road first. . . . so they wouldn't have to eat the other ones' dust going to Captiva."

Allen Nave
1992 Interview

The road near Island Inn in the 1940s, which was directly on the beach. (Courtesy John Veenschoten)

"... we'd tie two ski ropes on the side of the car, and one would drive the car sixty miles an hour up the beach, and ski right off the beach."

Edie Mugridge
1992 Interview

The dock in front of Bailey's General Store. The building and dock, like the Matthews Wharf preceding it, was destroyed by a hurricane—Donna in September 1960. At this writing, Donna is the most recent hurricane to hit the islands, an unprecedented respite of four decades.

147

The mailboat contract was taken over from the Kinzie steamers in 1936 by the Singleton Brothers, who ran the route until 1952. From 1952 until December 1964 when the contract expired, Palmer Ladd continued the mail and excursion service. In 1943 when the Reeds ended their postmaster tradition, a new location for the post office had to be chosen. Some islanders preferred the post office to be in Bailey's General Store at the mailboat landing, others favored the ferry landing. Captain Kinzie built a small building as a post office on his property and leased it to the government, ending the question. The mail continued to be delivered to Bailey's dock, where it was picked up and driven to the post office by the ferry dock for sorting and delivery.

Sanibel Refuge Manager Tom Wood used his plane, nicknamed the "Work Horse," to inspect refuges under his management from Tarpon Springs to the Keys. He used the pontoon plane to establish the direction of the refuge impoundment dikes in 1963. Emmy Lu Lewis remembered Wood piloting her to Tallahassee in the early 1960s to lobby the Internal Improvement Board to dedicate state lands to the refuge as "one of the happiest experiences I've ever had." (Courtesy J. N. "Ding" Darling National Wildlife Refuge)

The wooden Blind Pass bridge was replaced by a two-lane concrete bridge in 1954.

Before the east end canals were dug the interior wetlands periodically broke through the dunes to empty excess water from rainfall. The best-known "river mouth" was near the present Colony, shown here from the air. The tannin-stained rainwater flows into the Gulf and toward the east. Once the water pressure was relieved longshore currents and tidal action would close the break until the next event. When the canals were dug dams or weirs were placed so salt water would be separated from the freshwater system and now excess water is released or retained according to specific schedules.

"They built houses on those [cabbage palm] ridges because it would drive a pump and get water. See, it was all surface water. . . . We always had plenty of water."

Belton Johnson
1982 Interview

[My wife and I collected shells to sell to a dealer.] "He made lamps and crazy stuff out of them. Stuff nobody would have but tourists would buy."

John Peurifoy
1979 Interview

Shells were hauled away by the handfull and the sackfull. An old island joke used to be that the best Sanibel shelling was at the Georgia border. That's where the shells stuffed in the trunk started to stink, and were abandoned. Most tourists fly instead of drive home now, and no live shelling is permitted, so shelling has diminished in Valdosta.

Cars crowded the island and parked in the narrow road at the Sanibel Community House for the Shell Fair each year. The live shell exhibit is always popular, and one of the "duties" of refuge personnel (Tom Wood, manager and only employee) in 1955 was to dredge live specimens by boat for the aquariums.

Hallie Matthews (center) enters a 1950s Shell Fair. Her friend, Dr. Louise Perry, practiced medicine for fifteen years in Asheville, North Carolina. Dr. Perry and her husband first came to Sanibel in 1918, and found the island so lacking in conveniences they turned around to leave on the next steamer. But it would not return until the following day. The Perrys survived the night and decided to stay. In 1924 they built a home named Spindrift, near Casa Ybel Resort, where she started a marine lab two years later. She directed the Shell Fair for many years and co-authored a shell reference book. Her scientific studies and writing included many aspects of marine life. She dredged specimens, raised junonias in aquariums, named fifteen shells new to science in two years, and wrote reports on her findings. She also imported alligators to Sanibel from the Everglades when Sanibel's alligators seemed to be nearly wiped out by hunting, and assisted in tarpon research. When neighbors needed medical attention she provided it. A visitor trying to pay the doctor was informed, "We are glad to help each other on Sanibel for nothing." During the Second World War she ran a children's eye clinic, examining 1,346 children without charge.

The mailboat *Santiva* prepares to dock at Sanibel in the 1950s. Passengers on the mailboat could enjoy the trip downriver from Fort Myers from the roof seats or inside.

The *Santiva* left Fort Myers each morning except Sunday and returned in the late afternoon after picking up and delivering mail, passengers, and freight to its several stops including Punta Rassa, St. James City, Sanibel, and Captiva. A Sanibel visitor could disembark in the morning and reboard the boat as it returned in the afternoon, or spend several days on the islands if desired. Priscilla Murphy stands in the center of the photo.

Vincent Veenschoten carries his catch from Dewey's Marina on Tarpon Bay. (Courtesy John Veenschoten)

152

The *Algiers* was a Mississippi River car ferry turned into a luxurious home in the image of a paddleboat. Brought onto Sanibel in 1959 by Helen and Lathrop Brown, the 150-foot-long mansion was destined to sit empty and mysterious for twenty-three years. Lathrop Brown, a former congressman from New York and Franklin Roosevelt's college roommate and best man, died shortly after the boat conversion was completed. Mrs. Brown never lived in it. Dobermans roamed the grounds and a caretaker lived on the Gulf-front twenty-five acres. With thirteen rooms, five baths, enclosed decks, a restaurant kitchen, pool, gold bath fixtures and a Picasso on the wall, the *Algiers* might be considered a pioneer of the luxury houses which increasingly appear on the islands. Its feathered stacks were used by boaters as a landmark until the *Algiers* was bulldozed in 1982. Its acreage is now city-owned Gulfside Park.

The *Best* was also the first Kinzie ferry, and ran all thirty-five years of ferry operation from 1928 to 1963. It was later joined by the *Islander* (1939), a second (smaller) *Islander* (1947), the *Yankee Clipper* (1953) and the *Rebel* (1957). The causeway has now been open to vehicular traffic for longer than the ferries operated.

153

The juxtaposition of *Islander* and bridge construction in October 1962, is still resonant today. The old continues its daily routine while the new inexorably rises to shadow, and then block its path.

"People come down here because it's like it is. Then right off they want to go and change everything."

Sentiment of a longtime islander
Fort Myers News-Press article by Clare Taylor

"Practically all the people that's running the island is newcomers . . . They left where they was 'cause they didn't like it and come here. Just as soon as they get here they try to make it like the damn place they left. And it just irritates me all over the place."

John Peurifoy
1979 Interview

"It is always thus. We did it too and we all believed it was for the betterment of the Island. We thought we were saving the Island. Instead we keep diminishing its uniqueness."

Mary Bell
1998 Personal Communication

154

Chapter Seven

S anibel and Captiva remained isolated and peaceful, but changes were coming and islanders were attuned to the possibilities and dangers those changes might bring. Neighbors had always helped each other. The island was an extended family, in action and often in reality, through intermarriage. Volunteerism was not then labeled as such, but it is a long Sanibel tradition.

Confrontation and Conservation

Hurricane Donna roared out of the south in September 1960 and skirted the coast. Before the winds became too high, some islanders were evacuated by helicopter. Many others went to traditionally "safe" buildings to weather the blow with friends and family. Donna did considerable damage throughout Florida, and little help could be expected from outside the islands. After the storm islanders patrolled by boat to keep looters away while others worked to clear fallen casuarinas from the power lines and Periwinkle Way. Once power crews did arrive, they could begin restoring power more quickly. Many were without electricity for several weeks. The island school bus was commandeered for transport—despite the objections of the school authorities. Bailey's Store donated, and islanders cooked, all the store's meats for the workers. Seabathing was rampant. For weeks islanders coped, as they always had. Eventually power was restored and roofs were repaired.

New residents continued to be welcomed and brought into the community fold. Only certain people would make the trade-off of isolation, bad roads, mosquitoes, heat, storms, lengthy trips for doctor or shopping in return for wildlife, community, sun and beach, and escape from the "rat race." Those who did choose it cared about their community and its wildlife passionately. Clashes became inevitable between these islanders and outsiders who saw the islands as a recreational or economic resource rather than a special place.

Sanibel Planning and Zoning Authority was set up in 1959 with state approval. Lee Roy Friday later commented that it was the word *planning* that probably got the Board in trouble with county officials, but islanders could not countenance zoning without planning. A comprehensive land use plan for Sanibel was created. Conflicts about island road placement and developers' interests, and particularly whether Sanibel could supersede Lee County's authority on such issues, came to a head. The county eliminated the Sanibel Authority. Long-standing undercurrents of mistrust and conflict between the island and the county were reinforced even as the Sanibel Causeway was being built across San Carlos Bay.

Developer Hugo Lindgren had a vision for his Sanibel properties, but needed to attract more people to the island to sell that vision. Lindgren's vision was not shared by many islanders, and his partnership with the county in getting the causeway built was seen as another example of "them against us." He saw the causeway as a step forward for the islands. It would make living on the islands easier. He did not understand that an easier life was not islanders' first priority. Not only would Lindgren offer transportation to his customers, but he lobbied for adequate water supplies. In 1964, even before Greater Pine Island Water Association was incorporated, Lindgren contacted its principals about supplying water to Sanibel via pipeline. Island Water Association was formed in 1965. Lindgren donated property for the Sanibel-Captiva Chamber of Commerce at the "front door" to the island. Lindgren held right of approval for the building plans. The building would include an office for him with a separate entrance. All these actions benefited Lindgren, but he sincerely felt they also improved the islands.

In 1961 a weekly newspaper, the *Islander*, began publishing. The Sanibel Public Library was organized in 1963. In 1962 a modern school was built on San-Cap Road. It was voluntarily integrated, the first in the county. Philip and Ruth Hunter bought the old school and turned it into a community theater, the Pirate Playhouse. Sanibel National Wildlife Refuge was renamed for "Ding" Darling in 1967, and Sanibel-Captiva Conservation Foundation began its campaign to preserve other wildlife acreage.

As Lindgren foresaw, the causeway accelerated the islands' growth. Population increased, and the numbers of casual visitors skyrocketed. Condominiums began to rise, and apprehensions of an island resembling the east coast also rose. Developers damaged the clay seal separating the interior freshwater lens from surrounding salt water, and the specter of the destruction of Sanibel's unique wetlands arose. A six-weeks-long red tide in 1971 was followed by a tornado skipping across the island during tropical storm Agnes' passage offshore in 1972. Island isolation diminished a little further in 1973 when telephone calls to the mainland were longer toll calls. That year a second newspaper, the *Island Reporter*, began publishing. One of its first campaigns was to study the idea of incorporation, for both islands or Sanibel alone.

The struggle with the county to recognize what the islanders considered a special place wore on everyone. The idea of incorporation had floated below the surface for some time. By 1973, ten years after the causeway construction, a building boom was driving prices and numbers of buildings higher every week. In a single week the county issued Sanibel building permits whose value exceeded permit values for the entire previous year. More survey stakes appeared on the beach than sandpipers. But the question of incorporation also involved costs—of services, the conflict between ecology and economics, and the standing of the ordinary islander compared to wealthy owner-investors. There was much discussion and vacillation. Would city government really be any improvement over county rule?

When the incorporation referendum was taken in November 1974, it passed 689–394, with 85 percent of Sanibel's registered voters casting their ballot. A month later five council members were chosen from a field of sixteen: Porter Goss, Vernon MacKenzie, Zelda Butler, Charles LeBuff, and Francis Bailey. Top vote-getter Goss was chosen Sanibel's first mayor. The council members reflected

Sanibel's population—newcomers, oldtimers, business people, retired people, conservationists.

The City of Sanibel was in place, although lawsuits immediately challenged its very existence. One of Sanibel's first decisions was a building moratorium until a land-use plan was written and approved. Housing limits and environmental studies of all aspects of the island needed study. Protection of natural resources was a primary concern, although Mayor Goss also noted council did not want the island to become an exclusive enclave. The balance is difficult to maintain.

Longtime Sanibel resident and historian Mary Bell pointed out recently that "people come to the island because of the wildlife, but they stay because of the people." Sanibel history is the story of its people and their relationship to the island, whether for a day or a lifetime. So far the island has been fortunate, attracting people who care about their neighbors—the humans, animals, birds, plants and island itself. As Sanibel's present inevitably becomes its past, may that care and caring continue.

The *Yankee Clipper* glides to the dock on a glorious day. (Courtesy Marjorie Harris)

Bailey's General Store from the water. (Courtesy John Veenschoten)

After the Shanahan family lost the Palms Hotel in the disastrous 1936 fire, they converted a cottage on their property into their residence. Eventually daughter Snookie and son-in-law Jim Williams turned the cottage into a shell shop between the ferry landing and the lighthouse, an ideal location for the time. (Courtesy Al and Joy Dobbs)

The community of Wulfert had become a ghost town. A few board-and-batten buildings hid in the woods which had overgrown the fields and most of the citrus groves. Tomato fields became practice target ranges during World War II. Wulfert returned to the wild, dominated by gopher tortoises and joewood trees. Geologically the first and highest part of Sanibel, it seemed destined to remain a pristine ecological haven. (Courtesy Betty Anholt)

Casa Ybel's grass airfield hosted many small planes in its two-plus decades, but at 2600 feet was far too short to be a viable field once condominiums began to rise along West Gulf Drive. The FAA closed the field in 1979 after a series of accidents—one involving a plane cartwheeling across the road to land in a condo courtyard. This 1960 photo is of Dr. Charles and Vivian Pyke's Cessna, in which they visited the island a number of times. Cessnas were noted for their short-field landing capabilities. The Pykes would taxi in, register and carry their bags to one of the cottages on the grounds. Meals involved no choice of entree—everyone ate the same thing. (Courtesy Vivian Pyke)

A Lee County Mosquito Control DC-3 comes in at tree-top level to spray. Charles LeBuff recalls the time he saw the planes pass below him as he watched from the light-house tower. The early-morning appearance of the planes was greeted with relief by many islanders, although spraying became controversial due to perceived environmental effects. Mosquito Control Director T. Wayne Miller declared "chemical control of the adult mosquito is the poorest possible way to do it." The planes are seldom seen now, as helicopter larvaciding usually controls mosquito hatches. (Courtesy Betty Anholt)

"You know, there used to be the population of Sanibel—mosquitoes, cockroaches, and fleas."

Clarence Rutland
1968 Interview

"The year we were married (1933) and went over there [Sanibel], there were no paved roads, no electricity, no telephone, not much of anything except mosquitoes."

Ernest Kinzie
1989 Interview

Hurricane Donna in 1960 brought down Australian pines along the main road, and islanders spent weeks clearing it and electrical rights-of-way so the power company could restore power. The roof of the booth which houses the live shell exhibit at Shell Fairs, shown here, was damaged by a falling limb. (Courtesy Al and Joy Dobbs)

Hurricane Donna removed the roof from the Sea Gull
Cottage on the bay side of the island. Originally
owned by the George Miskimen family, it was purchased by the Dormers in later years. (Courtesy
Elinore Dormer)

"The only thing certain about hurricanes is that they are
always uncertain."

"You could feel the fear in the house during the hurricane
[Donna—1960]. Now wait a minute, it was the other way
around. When the barometer started to rise, that's when
you could feel, could realize how scared you were."

Francis Bailey
1973 Interview

A picnic at Esperanza's, Woodring Point. Picnics, fish fries, and oyster roasts were common get-togethers for islanders, winter residents and tourists alike. Whether in the mangroves, on the beach, under the lighthouse, at a resort, the Shell Fair or Legion Hall, such gatherings cemented friendships. (Courtesy Ralph Woodring)

The Bait Box in its 1970s trailer and outbuilding. From his shop owner Ralph Woodring booked shelling or fishing trips for his mother, Esperanza Woodring. Bay shrimp are caught nightly in Sanibel waters so island fishermen have early morning bait and fishing supplies. (Courtesy Betty Anholt)

Sanibel's Public Library began in a closet in the Community House, operating a couple of hours per week. Genevieve Cooper Muir, whose family had home-steaded along Tarpon Bay Road, cata-logued the books. The desk used for check-in and check-out was lent to the Sanibel Chamber of Commerce, also operating out of the Community House, when the Library was not open. Emmy Lu Read (Lewis) and Elise Fuller check out. (Courtesy Sanibel Public Library)

[The library] "operated out of a small room in the Sanibel Community Association, . . . probably 8 by 8 feet square. They had something like 350 volumes."

Robert C. Haynie
1979 Interview

Setting pilings for the causeway, 1963. One of the causeway islands, man-made, is visible in the distance. The causeway has caused significant changes in water flow in San Carlos Bay, and is often blamed for the demise of scallop fishing in the lower sound. However, in 1955, long before the causeway was built, Refuge Manager Tom Wood reported, "Bay scallops were non-existent. None were found and the commercial fishermen turned to other catches. No logical reason was given. Two years ago they were caught in quantities." (Courtesy Al and Joy Dobbs)

The official causeway opening ceremonies were held at the toll booths at Punta Rassa. Hugo Lindgren is standing at left rear. Lindgren became the central figure in the causeway controversy as he pushed for the bridge to be built. For him it was an economic decision, for others an emotional one. Many islanders believe building the causeway without the county's serious consideration of island residents' feelings was a major factor in establishing the City of Sanibel a decade later.

"... they [Lee County Commissioners] just sort of automatically were 'agin' anything that Sanibel proposed. I might say conversely, Sanibel was usually opposed to anything they proposed, as it affected our density and the aesthetic values we were trying to preserve. It was not a mutual admiration society."

Robert C. Haynie
1979 Interview

While the opening of the causeway was celebrated by officials, many islanders opted to be part of a farewell party for the ferries and the way of life which the causeway would forever change. The ferry ceased operation as soon as the causeway opened, although the mailboat continued operation until its contract ended in 1964. Mail addressed by a person's name alone, like this invitation to the ferry farewell, continued to be delivered well into the 1970s, as few streets were even named.

Colon Moore's dragline, perched on a lumber foundation so it wouldn't sink into the mud, digs the canal which provides the sand for the present refuge roadway. This photo is taken near the first culvert on the drive in May 1963, the same month the causeway opened. (Courtesy J. N. "Ding" Darling National Wildlife Refuge)

Dredge-and-fill became a dominant activity on Sanibel in the 1950s and 1960s, especially after the causeway connected the island to the mainland. Concern for the unusual island environment accelerated as more of the island was turned into subdivisions and lowlands were filled. Sanibel-Captiva Conservation Foundation formed in 1967. Its founding members had secured the mostly salt-water-oriented J. N. "Ding" Darling National Wildlife Refuge and turned to protecting the fresh-water interior of the island as well. SCCF now is the island's largest private land conservator. (Courtesy J. N. "Ding" Darling National Wildlife Refuge)

"The east coast of Florida was a startling example of what we did not want on Sanibel. . . . We started to search out ways where we could do something. We were so few of us then that if one got a headache, we all took some aspirin." [On 1950s Sanibel planning and zoning]

Lee Roy Friday
1981 Interview

The Library soon outgrew the Community House and moved to a storefront (shown here) next to the Sanibel Community Church. Standing in the truck: Pat Siegenthaler and Jerry Martin. Left to right: Elise Fuller, A. F. Coburn, Leon Levy, Willie Glass, Joyce White, Frances Heyser, Jo Pickens, Pauline Wilson, Edith Levy, and Don and Florence Simonds. Yet another move to larger quarters was followed by the donations of land by Gerald and Florence Martin (a relative of the homesteading Nutt family), allowing the Library to build its "permanent" building in 1973. (Courtesy Sanibel Public Library)

A residence in 1964 when photographed here, this building at the intersection of Island Inn Road and Tarpon Bay Road began as a Baptist church in 1919, intermittently became the schoolhouse for black children, and later became commercial property. (Courtesy Southwest Florida Historical Society)

In 1964 the old schoolhouse was abandoned. Notice the width and condition of Periwinkle Way. (Courtesy Southwest Florida Historical Society)

The Pirate Playhouse interior, 1965. When Ruth and Philip Hunter (shown) retired from their previous careers in show business to come to Sanibel, they immediately saw the empty school as a community theater and their home. After enclosing the front porch for a box office and other changes, they opened their first season in 1965 with "The Reluctant Debutante." Besides the Hunters and their daughter Robin, the cast included islanders Priscilla Murphy, Jane Hines, Roy Bazire, Jerry Muench, and Robert Dormer. (Courtesy Robin Hunter Karr)

Mario Hutton, remembered locally for his fishing prowess with friend Clarence Rutland and popular "photo-verse" programs, points to his part of the island in 1965 on the Chamber of Commerce billboard map. Born in Rome, Hutton's opposition to Mussolini's regime caused him difficulty in his native country. He obtained U.S. citizenship, served the U.S. Army in Criminal Investigation in Europe, and when the Huttons retired to Sanibel he became an articulate leader in local conservation. (Courtesy Mario Hutton)

Periwinkle Way, April 1965. A contrast with today's Easter vacation traffic. (Courtesy Mario Hutton)

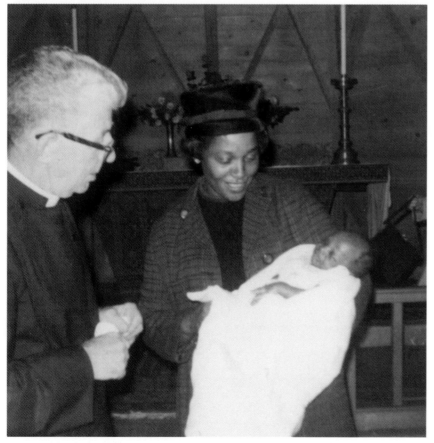

Father Thomas Madden of St. Michael & All Angels Episcopal Church stands with (Mrs. Carl) Mozella Jordan and newly baptized son Timothy in February 1966. A native of Scotland, the much-beloved priest came to Sanibel when Episcopal services were being held at Casa Marina Restaurant. When Hurricane Donna ripped off its roof, church construction was necessary, and completed in 1961. Tim, a fourth-generation islander, holds the distinction of being the first black congregant baptized. (Courtesy Mozella Jordan)

Charlotte Kinzie White, Roy Bazire, and Priscilla Murphy at a Pirate Playhouse production. Charlotte White's family ran the Kinzie Boat Line including the ferries and earlier steamers, and her husband later served as mayor. Roy Bazire was first director of Sanibel-Captiva Conservation Foundation and an ardent conservationist; and Priscilla Murphy established the islands' first real estate company. (Courtesy Jean Culpepper)

"Roy Bazire . . . suggested that our next move should be to buy some of the wetlands in the center of Sanibel. His friend, Dr. Craighead, . . . was very impressed with the Sanibel wetlands and the ecological importance of them."

Emmy Lu Lewis
1979 Interview

The last of the Gulfside docks, this structure stood near Shell Basket Lane until the late 1960s. (Courtesy Mario Hutton)

Looking down Periwinkle Way toward the Lighthouse about 1970. The causeway enters
Shell Harbor, while gulfside is Beachview subdivision with its diverted freshwater canal,
nicknamed the Panama Canal because it was dug so wide and deep. The horseshoe-
shaped cleared subdivision is Sanibel Lake Estates, next to the Pirate Playhouse. Casa
Ybel Road is prominent to the right, paralleling Periwinkle.

Red tide is a periodic natural phenomenon on Florida's west coast, a bloom of a dinoflagellate which suffocates much ocean life in its path, also creating respiratory problems for people. The most severe red tide recorded on Sanibel was in 1947, and a six-week-long 1971 outbreak piled windrows of dead fish on the beaches. They had to be disposed of by county bulldozers digging trenches on the beach to bury the rotting tons of fish. In 1996 manatees became the major victims of a spring red tide, which killed an estimated 10 percent of the vicinity's sea cows. (Courtesy of *Islander*)

Most island resorts provided cooking facilities for shell collectors so they could clean and display their collections.

Volunteer Sylvia Strong reads to a group of summer Story
Hour children in 1971. This leased quarters on Periwinkle
Way, third of the five Library locations, was followed by
the Library's "own" building in 1973. (Courtesy Sanibel
Public Library)

The 1971 Beach Road weir closes off the Sanibel river or slough system from the complex of salt-water canals cut into the east end of Sanibel. Fresh-water can no longer overflow into the Gulf of Mexico as it had in the past. (Courtesy Island Water Association)

In June of 1972 islanders were surprised by a tornado which spun off from Agnes, a passing tropical storm. The tornado crossed the island at its widest part, touching down near Casa Ybel, then destroying a row of storefronts next to the Community Church on its way to ripping the porch from the Woodring home on their point. (Courtesy Jean Culpepper)

Elementary school Christmas programs were a staple at the
Community House well into the 1970s. These 1973 third-
graders include Morganna Anholt, Robin Pickens, Eric
Wightman, (back) Manuela Eschbaum, Tommy Morse,
and Beth Holland. (Courtesy Suzanne Pickens)

Mada Harrison, Sanibel-Captiva Conservation Foundation Board member, plants native shrubs at the Sanibel Public Library in 1973. SCCF established a native plant nursery under the direction of Norma Jeanne Byrd, who locally pioneered the use of Florida native plants for landscape uses. (Courtesy Sanibel Public Library)

Moving in, 1973. While Carl Jordan is busy aligning book-
shelves, Robin Pickens' job of filling shelves gets side-
tracked. After a series of additions to this library was out-
grown, a new building opened next to City Hall in 1994.
(Courtesy Sanibel Public Library)

Sanibel's first City Hall was a crowded space at Periwinkle Place shopping center. At this council meeting, clockwise around the table from left: Assistant City Attorney Roger Berres, Councilman Charles LeBuff, Mayor Porter Goss, unknown, Ed Olling, unknown, Alice Kyllo, Paul Howe, Councilwoman Zelda Butler, Councilman Francis Bailey, City Manager Dave Bretzke. Standing: Duane White, John Kontinos, Arthur Hunter. Seated: Jim Robson, Bill Frye, Ann Winterbotham. Councilman Vernon MacKenzie is off-camera to left. (Courtesy *Island Reporter*)

Lee County Deputy Lou Secary serves Sanibel Mayor
Porter Goss a summons as City Manager Bill Nungester
looks on in 1976. The newly formed City of Sanibel faced
several challenges in its early months. A Naples developer
filed suit challenging the city's legality in April 1975. It
claimed the City of Sanibel did not meet the density
requirements for incorporation as set forth by the State
legislature. The suit prevented bank financing to permit
City operation until tax revenues would begin to flow, and
bankruptcy loomed. Sanibel citizens rushed to lend the
new city $250,000 in bonds to allow it to continue operat-
ing. (Courtesy *Island Reporter*)

Selected Bibliography

Numerous periodicals and government records have been consulted for this book. Some particularly useful ones include back issues of such journals as *Tequesta* and *Florida Historical Quarterly*. Newspapers like the *Fort Myers Press, Fort Myers Tropical News, Fort Myers News-Press, Islander* (1934–1937), *Sanibel-Captiva Islander, Island Reporter*, and newsletters, contain an abundance of information for the patient researcher. U.S. and Florida Census Records, Lee County Land Records, and many maps and nautical charts from different periods have been studied. Masters theses have been useful.

A large number of oral histories have been taped and transcribed on the island in the last thirty years. All have been read and listened to, often several times. Descendants have provided additional illumination through personal communication.

A number of books and an abundance of articles on Florida history, archaeology, geology and environment relate to Sanibel in whole or part. Many of these have been consulted, especially those covering local history in the southwest Florida region and Charlotte Harbor. A small sampling of the books follow. The subdivisions are artificial and do interrelate—history is a part of environment, and environment informs archaeology.

GEOLOGY AND ENVIRONMENT

Henry, James A. et. al. *The Climate and Weather of Florida*, Pineapple Press, 1994.

Hoffmeister, John Edward. *Land from the Sea, the Geologic Story of Florida*, University of Miami Press, 1974.

Odum, William E. et. al. *The Ecology of the Mangroves of South Florida: A Community Profile*, U.S. Fish and Wildlife Services, 1982.

Randazzo, Anthony F. and Douglas S. Jones, Eds. *The Geology of Florida*, University Press of Florida, 1997.

Soil Survey of Lee County, Florida, U.S. Department of Agriculture Soil Conservation Service, 1981.

Tannehill, Ivan Ray. *Hurricanes, Their Nature and History*, Princeton University Press, 1945.

ARCHAEOLOGY

Brown, Robin C. *Florida's First People*, Pineapple Press, 1994.

Cushing, Frank H. "Explorations of Ancient Key Dwellers' Remains on the Gulf Coast of Florida," *Proceedings of the American Philosophical Society*, XXXV, 1897.

Fontaneda, Hernando d'Escalante. *Memoir* translation by Buckingham Smith, editor, David O. True, University of Miami, 1945.

Hann, John H. *Missions to the Calusa*, University of Florida Press, 1991.

Marquardt, William H., ed. *Culture and Environment in the Domain of the Calusa*, Institute of Archaeology and Paleoenvironmental Studies, Monograph Number 1, University of Florida, 1992.

SANIBEL AND REGIONAL HISTORY

Anholt, Betty. *The Trolley Guide to Sanibel and Captiva Islands*, private printing, 1990.

Brown, Canter, Jr. *Florida's Peace River Frontier*, University of Central Florida Press, 1991.

Carter, Clarence E., ed. *Territorial Papers of the United States, Florida Territory*, Vols. 22–26. Washington, 1957–1962.

Clark, John R. *The Sanibel Report*, The Conservation Foundation, 1976.

Dimock, A. W. and Julian A. *Florida Enchantments*, Outing Publishing Co., 1908.

Dormer, Elinore. *The Sea Shell Islands*, Vantage Press, 1975.

Douglas, Marjory Stoneman. *The Everglades, River of Grass*, Pineapple Press, rev. ed. 1988.

Fritz, Florence. *The Unknown Story of Sanibel and Captiva*, McClain Printing Co., 1974.

Gatewood, George. *Ox Cart Days to Airplane Era in Southwest Florida*, private printing, 1939.

_____. *On Florida's Coconut Coasts*, Punta Gorda Herald, 1944.

LeBuff, Charles. *Sanybel Light: An Historical Autobiography*, Amber Publishing, 1998.

Mueller, Edward A. *Steamships of the Two Henrys*, private printing, 1996.

Pearse, Eleanor H. D. *Florida's Vanishing Era*, private printing, 1954.

Stone, Donald O. and Beth W. Carter. *The First 100 Years: Lee County Public Schools 1887–1987*, 1987.

The WPA Guide to Florida. Pantheon Books, 1939, 1967.

About the Author

Betty Anholt, after visiting Florida (and Sanibel) since childhood, moved here with her husband Jim and two children in the late 1960s to become year-round residents. Her interests in Florida ecology and history led her into research, volunteer work, and writing in the fields.

Betty has published poetry and articles both regionally and nationally. Her book, *The Trolley Guide to Sanibel and Captiva Islands*, was published in 1991. Betty is a graduate of Rutgers University.

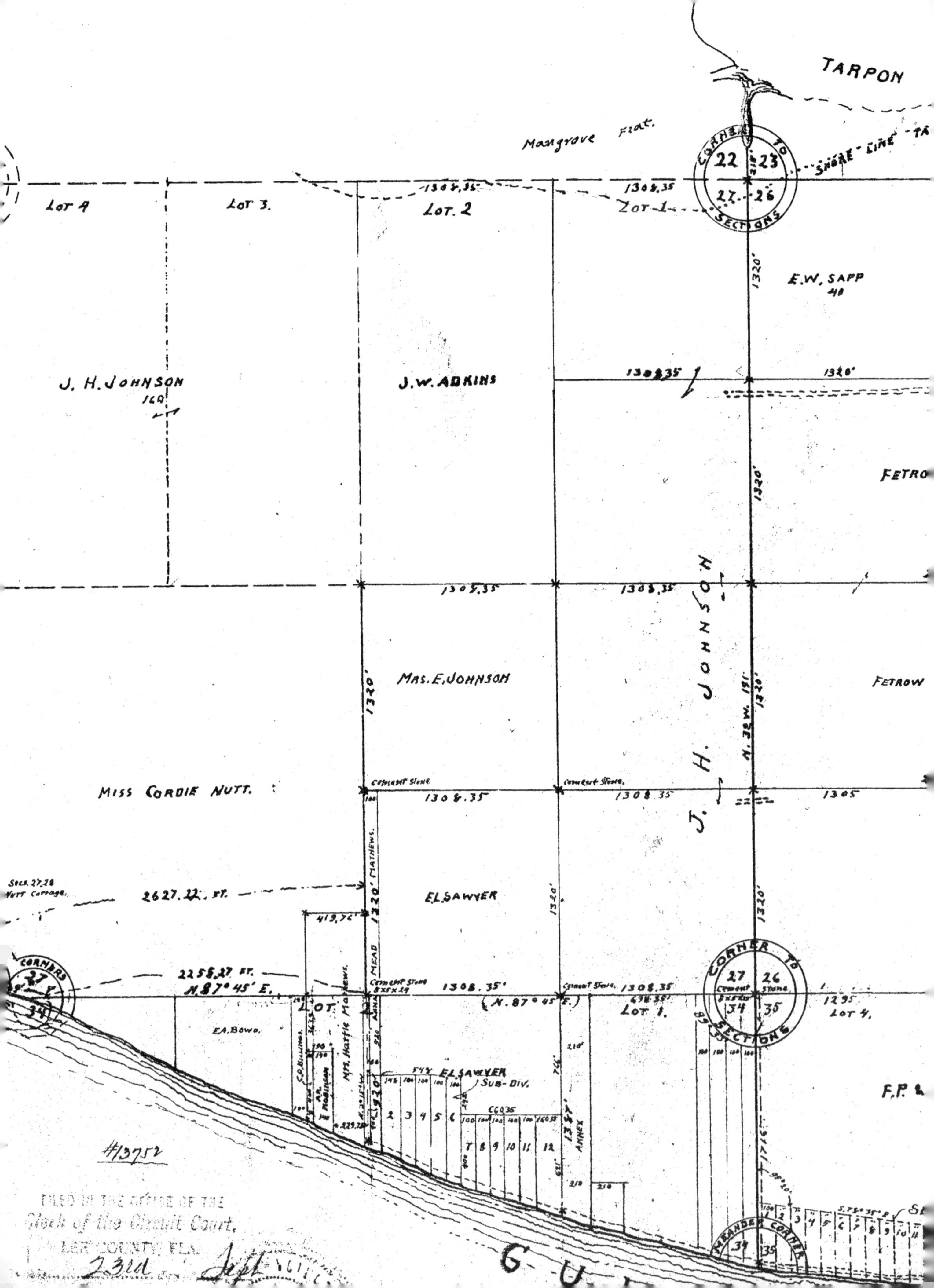

TARPON
Mangrove Flat.
SHORE LINE
CORNER TO SECTIONS
22 23 27 26
LOT 4
LOT 3.
LOT. 2
LOT 1
1308.35
E.W. SAPP
40
J. H. JOHNSON
160
J.W. ADKINS
1320'
FETROW
MRS. E. JOHNSON
J. H. JOHNSON
MISS CORDIE NUTT.
Cement Stone
1305
Secs. 27.28
Nutt Cottage
2627.22 FT.
ELSAWYER
419.76
MEAD
MATHEWS
CORNERS
2258.27 FT.
N.87° 45' E.
(N. 87° 45' E.)
LOT
LOT 1.
LOT 4.
1295
E.A. Bowd.
C.D. Billings
A.R. Robinson
Mrs. Hattie Mathews
ELSAWYER
SUB-DIV.
1 2 3 4 5 6
7 8 9 10 11 12
ANNEX
1387'
1716'
F.P.
CORNER TO 27 26 34 35 SECTIONS
MEANDER CORNER
34 35
1 2 3 4 5 6 7 8 9 10 11
#13752
FILED IN THE OFFICE OF THE
Clerk of the Circuit Court,
23rd
Sept
G U